IT TAKES RESPECT

IT TAKES RESPECT

AENEAS WILLIAMS

Multnomah Publishers *Sisters, Oregon*

IT TAKES RESPECT
published by Multnomah Publishers, Inc.

© 1998 by Aeneas Williams

International Standard Book Number: 1-57673-453-6
Printed in the United States of America

Cover photography by Jessen Associates
Cover design by Stephen Gardner

Scripture quotations are from *The Holy Bible,* New International Version (NIV)
© 1973, 1984 by International Bible Society, used by permission of
Zondervan Publishing House.

Also quoted, *Revised Standard Version Bible* (RSV) © 1946, 1952 by the Division of
Christian Education of the National Council of the Churches of Christ in the
United States of America.

Multnomah is a trademark of Multnomah Publishers, Inc. and is registered
in the U.S. Patent and Trademark Office.
The colophon is a trademark of Multnomah Publishers, Inc.

For information:
Multnomah Publishers, Inc.•PO Box 1720•Sisters, Oregon 97759

LIBRARY OF CONGRESS CATALOGING-IN-PUBLICATION DATA
Williams, Aeneas, 1968-
    It takes respect/Aeneas Wiliams
    p. cm.
    ISBN 1-57673-453-6 (alk. paper)
    1. Williams, Aeneas, 1968-   2. Football players
United States—Biography.   3. Football players—Religious life—
United States   4. Christian life.   I. Title.
GV939.W485A3 1998
796.332'092—dc21
    [B]   98-19526
                                                CIP

98 99 00 01 02 03 04 05 — 10 9 8 7 6 5 4 3 2 1

This book is dedicated to my parents, Lawrence and Lillian Williams, who instilled in me the principles of hard work, discipline, respect, and responsibility, as a foundation for being a productive person. For their lives and sacrifice, I am grateful. I would not be where I am today if they had not encouraged me to be and do my very best.

I also dedicate this book to my wife, Tracy, who has stood with me in every endeavor I have attempted. We have learned that when we work together there is nothing we can't accomplish. She is my friend, my partner, and my confidante. I thank God for her and her willingness to stand with me.

TABLE OF CONTENTS

Humble yourselves before the Lord,
and he will lift you up.
JAMES 4:10

INTRODUCTION

As an American citizen, a father and a husband, and a Christian man, I've grown alarmed over what I'm seeing take place in our culture in the 1990s. I'm especially concerned about what is happening to our youth.

I'm not talking about specifics such as crime, drug and alcohol abuse, sexually transmitted diseases, or unwanted and unplanned pregnancies. These are big problems, to be sure. But they are just symptoms of what I see as the bigger problem we face as we head toward the new millennium.

What is that problem? It is what I see as a deeply held disdain in our culture for authority. It is the spirit that says, "I'll do what I want, when I want, and with whom I want." It's a way of thinking that says we don't have to answer to anybody.

Simply put, it's a lack of respect for the institutions that God has put in place to guide us, motivate us, and at times, restrain us.

We Americans don't like to be told what to do. We don't like living by rules, and we don't like having someone in authority over us. We don't like the idea of submission or accountability. We like to do what we want regardless of the consequences.

We don't respect authority of any kind. Consequently, our culture has become like that in the Old Testament time of the Judges where, "every man did what was right in his own eyes" (Judges 17:6, RSV).

The consequences of our lack of respect for authority are all around us. And things are only getting worse. Sure, we may throw some money at the symptoms, and things might get better in the short run. But our efforts offer only temporary relief from the symptoms. In the long run, our problems only come back at us with more ferocity than ever before.

Our efforts to solve our problems make me think of the futile efforts of a custodian who kept mopping up the water off of a restroom floor without fixing the leaky toilet. No matter how hard he worked, it was never long before the floor was flooded again.

Right now our nation is at flood stage. Worse than that, we won't even let the custodian in to fix the problem.

Man's rebellion against authority isn't new. We've been fighting authority since Adam and Eve fell into original sin. And as we get closer to Christ's return, I believe we'll see our rebellion against God and earthly authority become more and more pronounced.

I've written this book to tell you—to *show* you—that there's a better way to deal with this in our personal lives. I've written this book to show you that there is nothing wrong with respecting authority and submitting to it. Not only is there nothing wrong with respecting authority, the Word of God commands it, and it's for our own good.

As you read this book, I want you to see that God has blessed me in many ways simply because I'm willing to respect the authority figures He's placed in my life. To tell you the truth, I feel doubly blessed because I believe He's worked in my life so that I *want* to respond respectfully to those who are in authority over me, and I've actually *chosen* to make certain individuals authority figures in my life.

How has God blessed me, you ask? Let me start with the part of my life you may already know about: my career. God has blessed me by helping me to become one of the most respected defensive backs in the National Football League. If that wasn't enough, He's also blessed me with an incredible ministry with my teammates and friends. Oh yes, I also have a beautiful, loving, godly wife and the sweetest little daughter I could ever have hoped for.

While not everybody will be blessed with a career in the National Football League—in fact, very few people are—I know that God has a plan for each and every one of His people who are fully submitted to His will for their lives. I know that He wants each of us to accomplish great things for Him in our own corner of the world.

You might look at me and think there's no way you can do the kinds of things I do for God. But you can. You see, the strength I have through my faith isn't because I've anything special. It's because I'm submitted to God and to the authority He has placed over me. It's because I've humbled myself and allowed God to do what He wants with me and in me.

I'm a living example of what Jesus said in John 15:5: "Apart from me you can do nothing." Without Him, I never would have been able to accomplish what I have—as a football player, as a husband and father, and as a servant of God. None of the blessings I've received would have come had I not fully committed myself to Jesus Christ and humbly asked Him to do with me as He pleases.

It's not hard for me to submit to authority, because God has continually brought strong, caring authority figures into my life. From the time I was a child living in New Orleans with my mother and father until now, as a player in the National Football League, I've always been surrounded by strong, positive authority figures.

I realize that not everybody has been blessed with good authority figures in their lives like I've been. Some have seen nothing but negative authority figures. Because of that, too many people—some of them Bible-believing Christians—don't want anything to do with authority. They want to go and do it their own way.

I'm here to tell you that won't work.

The Bible tells us that earthly authority is God's plan to protect our lives and to give us direction. You see, God could very easily have just let us go and said, "You're on your own." But He loved us too much to do that. He loved us so much that He sent His only Son to die for us so that we could have a personal relationship with the ultimate in a loving authority figure: God Himself!

God hasn't put authority figures in this world just to keep us down or to keep track of us. He gives us authority figures because He loves us and wants the best for us. He wants to give us direction and discipline in our lives, and earthly authority is how He does it.

I want you to know you don't have to go it alone in your faith. I want you to see through my life that there is nothing better than living a life that is submitted to God and to the people He brings into your life as authority figures.

I want you to see what God can do in the life of an ordinary guy from New Orleans when he decides to lay aside his selfish pride and submit himself.

Most of all, I want you to see what He too can do in your life.

WILL I STAY OR WILL I GO?

SUBMITTING TO GOD'S WILL

> *Teach me to do your will,*
> *for you are my God;*
> *may your good Spirit*
> *lead me on level ground.*
>
> —PSALM 143:10

"Man, are you out of your mind?"
"What could you possibly have been thinking?"
"You should have gotten out while the gettin' was good!"

Those are some of the comments I heard after I had decided to stay with the Arizona Cardinals after my two-year contract, my second pact with the team, expired following the 1995 season.

I became what is called an unrestricted free agent after that season, and under the National Football League's agreement with the NFL Players Association I had the right to sign with any team that bid for my services without having to worry about the Cardinals matching the offer and retaining my services.

In other words, I was free to go where I wanted.

Given the state of the Cardinals team that season, most people thought I should have bolted.

Believe me, I thought about it myself.

I'll put it bluntly: The Arizona Cardinals had a rough year in 1995, Coach Buddy Ryan's second—and last—with the team, finishing a disappointing 4-12 after a promising 8-8 record under Coach Ryan in 1994.

Sure, there were some close losses along the way, but there were some blowouts, too. The bottom line is that we just didn't play very well. We finished at or near the bottom of the league in just about every major statistical category both offensively and defensively. It seemed like we were going to have to start over in our quest to become a winner.

When the 1995 season ended, team owner and president Bill Bidwell fired Coach Ryan and hired Vince Tobin who had worked the previous two seasons as defensive coordinator of the Indianapolis Colts. Coach Tobin came in with some impressive credentials, having received the credit for rebuilding a Colts' defense that was ranked last in the NFL in 1993 before improving to seventh in 1995, when Indianapolis came within one dropped desperation pass of beating the Pittsburgh Steelers for the AFC championship and a berth opposite the Dallas Cowboys in Super Bowl XXX.

It was a major change of direction for the Cardinals, but the question for me was, would I be around to see the changes?

I had a decision to make.

Moving On?

I'd been blessed with a good season in 1995. I finished with six interceptions—two of which I returned for touchdowns—and was selected as a starter in the Pro Bowl for the second straight year. My six picks that season gave me fifteen over two seasons, the most of any player in the league over that time span. In addition, I was a consensus first-team All-Pro at cornerback.

If you guessed that my credentials over those two seasons got me a lot of attention from other teams in the league when my contract expired, you're right. I was then one of the top free agents in the market—certainly the top cornerback in a year where cornerbacks were a hot commodity in the NFL. That season alone, quality corners such as Phillippi Sparks, Eric Davis, Troy Vincent, Ashley Ambrose, Dale Carter, and Super Bowl XXX Most Valuable

Player Larry Brown were free agents looking for big contracts.

Close to half the teams in the league contacted me to express interest or to make offers. Several of the teams who called were playoff contenders, and a couple of them had Super Bowl potential.

My wife, Tracy, and I didn't even bother to visit some of the teams who called because we knew in our hearts that God wasn't calling us to go with them. A few of them I wouldn't have minded checking out, but I knew it was better not to put myself in the path of temptation when I already knew that God didn't want me there.

The only team we ended up visiting was the Jacksonville Jaguars, who offered me a five-year contract. The offer from the Jaguars was very appealing to me, both because of the terms and because Jacksonville, while it was a first-year expansion team in 1995, was a franchise that was quickly on the rise. The Jaguars had won four games their first year, which was no small accomplishment. They had been competitive in all but one of their games.

The Jaguars had already signed several quality free agents in the off-season, and they'd had a strong draft, taking Kevin Hardy of the University of Illinois who was considered to be the best linebacker coming out that year and the second pick overall. They had also picked up running back Natrone Means who had been waived earlier but was still a high quality player.

I could see that Jacksonville was a team with a lot of potential and potential that could be realized sooner rather than later. As it turned out, the team made it to the AFC championship game in 1996, their second season in existence. I really liked the idea of playing for a young team with so much promise.

More than anything, though, I wanted to be in the center of God's will. I wanted to know I was going where He wanted me to go and doing what He wanted me to do. I had submitted myself to doing His will, and if Jacksonville was where He wanted me, great! I was ready to sign. But if He wanted me to stay put and play for the Cardinals, I was willing to do just that.

It was time for my wife and I to seek God's direction.

Seeking Direction

Tracy and I prayed about our decision—together and separately—and talked through every aspect of it. We sought godly counsel from people we respected as men and women of God.

We also gave a lot of thought to what we would be leaving behind if we signed with another team.

We considered how God had used both of us in the lives of my teammates and their wives. We thought about the tremendous spiritual growth we had seen taking place in the lives of people God had given us the privilege of ministering to.

Finally we had to ask ourselves the key question: Did we believe God had finished what He had started through us in Phoenix? We both agreed that the answer to that question was a resounding no.

Tracy and I both knew that we should stay in Phoenix and continue the ministry that God had started through us there. Finally, on a Monday in late February, I signed a new five-year contract with the Cardinals.

One Tough Decision

The decision to stay with the Arizona Cardinals was a tough one for both Tracy and me. I have to be honest and tell you that my flesh fought with what we had decided to do—what we *knew* God wanted us to do. The money wasn't the issue; it was the part of me that wanted to go to a team that had a chance to win right away—a chance to go to the playoffs and win the Super Bowl—if not right now, then in the near future.

The bigger issue for me, though, was that I wanted more than anything to be in a place where God could make the best use of me. I was submitted to His will, even if His will meant leaving the NFL forever. I wanted to win on the football field, but I had a stronger, deeper desire in my heart. It was the desire to see completed what had been started in my friends and brothers on the Arizona Cardinals team.

Tracy and I thought and prayed and when we finally took everything into account, we knew there was no way we could leave. We both knew that God could have brought in somebody else to complete what had been started, but we also knew that He had no intention of doing that. He wanted us to stay put.

Changing Circumstances

I took a lot of flak for resigning with the Cardinals. The media ridiculed me and said I'd made a big mistake. One columnist even said I must have been crazy to resign when I easily could have flown the coop and gone to a winning team or a team with immediate winning potential. People who are close to me didn't understand why I stayed either. Even my dad couldn't understand why I'd do that. He had been hoping I'd sign with a contender.

There's no question that what Tracy and I did just before the 1996 season went against the conventional wisdom for free agents in the National Football League. To tell you the truth, if I were on the outside looking in at my situation, I'd probably have thought it was a little crazy myself.

But I knew I would have given up far more than winning a Super Bowl was worth if I had left the Cardinals.

I would never criticize someone who left his team and went somewhere where he had a chance to win. Reggie White took a tremendous amount of criticism for his decision to leave the Philadelphia Eagles and sign with the Green Bay Packers. (Never mind the fact that the Packers weren't yet a Super Bowl quality team when Reggie signed with them prior to the 1993 season.) Reggie said at the time that God had directed him to go to the Packers and that they would win a Super Bowl while he was there. A lot of people questioned Reggie's motives for moving on when he did. While it's not my place to question another man's heart, I will say that I respect Reggie White, and I believe that he was doing what God had directed him to do.

I understand wanting to win. I want to win just as much as any player in the NFL. But I also understand that when you are trying to live a life that is fully submitted to the will of God, there is danger in focusing only on criteria like money or whether your team is winning. Your first focus must be on doing what God wants you to do, even if it means going to a team that could finish 0-16.

I know that God can use players who have been brought into the lime-light because they've won the Super Bowl. But I also know that God doesn't need me to win a single game in order to use me. He can glorify Himself through me if my team never wins another game and if I never get another interception.

I realized when I was praying about where to go prior to the 1996 season that I couldn't allow temporary circumstances—in this case, playing for a team with a losing record—to influence my decision. I was well aware when I signed with Arizona in 1996 that the Cardinals had gone a long time with-out having a winning record. But I also had no question in my mind that I was called to stay in Arizona.

I resigned with Arizona because I knew that God wanted to continue my ministry here. I'm happy to report that my ministry is still growing and thriv-ing. I know beyond any doubt that I made the right decision.

Growing Pains

As a man of God and as a football player, I know that I am responsible to my Lord and to my employer, the Arizona Cardinals, to do all I can, not only to help my team win football games, but to be the best it can possibly be.

I have always given the best effort I could in practice, in games, and during the off-season but the results weren't what I or my coaches or my teammates—or the Arizona Cardinals' fans—had hoped for. During my first five years with the Cardinals, the team had a combined 29-53 record with our best season a .500 finish in 1994. We finished 4-12 during three of those seasons.

It hasn't always been easy for me to endure the losing, but God taught me during that time the importance of keeping my eyes on what I'm headed for and not on what I'm going through in the present. He taught me the importance of focusing on the eternal and on why He wanted me to stay here in the first place.

I have also realized that the trials I and my teammates have gone through are, in the long run, good for us. I've certainly gone through some trying times since I've been with the Cardinals, but I've grown through the tough times. I've become more mature as a football player, as a person, and as a man of God.

There have been times when it's been hard to understand why it has to be this way. I want to win. There isn't a player in this league who doesn't want to win. We're all very competitive people, and I think I'm one of the most competitive in the league. Without that will to win, I wouldn't have been in the league in the first place. But I've found that a player who can persevere through the tough times—including dealing with a losing situation—has a chance to succeed in the long run. To me, that's the attitude of a winner.

And it's the attitude of many successful teams of the nineties. It has had to be.

A lot of the great teams in the past decade have gone through times when they've struggled—some very recently. For example, the Green Bay Packers went through a 4-10 season in 1991—and several losing seasons before that—before they started their steady ascent from perennial loser to playoff contender to NFC championships in 1996 and 1997 and the Super Bowl XXXI championship in 1996. The Dallas Cowboys went through similar growing pains, finishing a dreadful 1-15 in 1989, then going on to win three Super Bowls in the '90s.

We on the Arizona Cardinals team have gone through more than our share of struggles, but we've always kept the faith and believed that there are better things ahead. We still believe that will happen.

But how will that happen? It will happen when I and my teammates start to make it happen. It's what we're paid to do. It's why I play professional football.

I believe that my decision to stay with the Arizona Cardinals will pay off for me with some on-the-field success. I believe that in the next few years you'll see some big improvements in our record. And I believe those improvements will come sooner rather than later.

But you know something? Even if we went 4-12 every year for the rest of my career—and I don't believe that will happen—I know that I made the right decision to stay here. God has already blessed me in ways that I wouldn't trade for all the Super Bowl rings ever made.

God has blessed me by allowing me to see men come to Jesus Christ. He's blessed me by allowing me to see hurting men healed. He's blessed me by allowing me to see men start to live godly lives. He's blessed me by allowing me to see damaged marriages getting repaired as men turn their lives over to God and submit to Him. Best of all, He's blessed me by giving me the privilege of making a difference in the lives of these men. He's blessed me by using me in their lives.

And He's blessed me for one reason: I was willing to submit to Him and to do His will.

For me, that's a way of life.

PASS COVERAGE

1. What do you do when you have a big decision to make? Do you pray? Do you seek counsel?

2. Has God ever prompted you to make a decision that others thought was strange? How did you respond?

3. How important is it to God that you give your best effort to be successful in an earthly pursuit (for example, winning at sports)?

4. In what ways does God encourage you when things don't go the way you want them to?

LEARNING RESPECT FROM MOM AND DAD

SETTING THE STANDARD EARLY

Honor your father and your mother, so that you may live long
in the land the LORD your God is giving you.
—EXODUS 20:12

Time after time, God has shown me the value of honoring authority, of submitting myself to Him and to the earthly authority figures He has brought into my world.

I learned those things early. I learned the basics of respecting authority when I was a kid growing up in New Orleans. Sure, God would later take me through some of life's fires so that what I knew would be tested and refined, but being raised by Lawrence and Lillian Williams, my dad and mom, built in me a foundational respect for authority.

I grew up in the house my father bought in 1972. I was four years old. That house, which my parents still call home, is located less than a mile from the campus of Tulane University in what would probably be considered a middle-class neighborhood by New Orleans' standards.

The home that Mom and Dad provided was a haven from a sometimes rough outside world for us three boys—my oldest brother, Malcolm; my middle brother, Achilles; and me. Our neighborhood wasn't what you would consider a ghetto, but there was enough going on that our parents had good reason to keep a sharp eye on us.

In New Orleans we didn't have problems with gangs, at least not the same kinds of problems that plague so many of the major cities across the country. That doesn't mean that we don't have problems with youth violence, though. New Orleans is divided into wards—wards are similar to precincts or districts in other cities—and there are often rivalries between youths in the different wards. It's not like kids are shooting each other over "turf" on a street corner, but there is violence between youths from rival wards. I can still remember seeing a young boy getting shot simply for trying to help his brother who had gotten into a fight.

I saw my friends getting themselves into plenty of trouble as I was growing up. It was hard not to see those things, because I not only lived in the neighborhood, I also went to what lots of people in New Orleans thought was the worst junior high and high school in the city.

I'm not about to tell you I was a perfect kid; I did some things that I knew were wrong. I messed up plenty. But I had a sense of limits at that time in my life, a sense of right and wrong. That is sense I learned at home with Mom and Dad.

Learning to Toe the Line at Home

The biggest difference between me and some of the kids I knew growing up—kids who got in a lot more trouble than I did—wasn't that I was any better than they were. It wasn't that I had some innate sense of right and wrong that they lacked. The difference was my parents, pure and simple. Mom and Dad knew about the problems that were out there, and they were determined to keep their three sons from getting into the kind of trouble that so many of our friends and neighbors were getting into.

Considering the circumstances, Mom and Dad were the best parents I could have had.

I didn't grow up in what you would consider a "Christian" home. Mom and Dad didn't go to church—although they made us boys go to church for a time when I was a kid—and there really wasn't much talk of God in our home. (I'm happy to report, however, that Mom and Dad have since given their lives to Christ.)

Somehow, though, Mom and Dad had the kind of wisdom and smarts they needed to pass along a strong sense of morality to their sons.

They did that for us for one reason: they loved us and wanted us to grow up to be the best young men we could possibly be.

So many of my neighbors and friends had parents who didn't seem to care about them—or if they did care, they certainly didn't know how to show it. My parents were as far from that as could be. Dad and Mom were always there for us three boys, giving us the kind of guidance a kid needs growing up.

Dad and Mom made their boys their top priority in life, and we could see that in the way they took an interest in the things we did. I can't remember too many times when they—along with my aunts (Dad's sisters)—didn't show up for an event in which we were participating. If we had a baseball or football game, they were always there giving us encouragement and support.

I look back with deep, deep gratitude when I think about what I had growing up. Dad and Mom could have been like so many other parents we knew back then—out doing other things and not paying enough attention to their kids. But they were always there for us, even when it was a challenge—even when *we* were the challenge.

Home by Dark

My parents were very protective and strict when it came to me and my brothers. They knew about the dangers to our safety, and they understood that there were temptations to do the wrong things out on the streets. They especially understood about the temptations that lay in wait for a kid after the sun goes down.

Like most young kids, I wanted to stay out late with my friends. Mom and Dad, though, wouldn't have any of that. They always insisted that I be in the house at a reasonable hour even during the summer when I had no homework to do.

Had it been up to me, I would have been out until well past midnight, but that just wasn't going to happen in the Williams home. I had a hard time with that. I couldn't understand why I couldn't stay outside with my buddies. As far as I was concerned, there couldn't have been a good reason for it. I just thought my parents were being overprotective—and boring.

As an adult, I look back on Mom and Dad with a new, God-given understanding. Now I see how my parents dealt with me as an example of what the Bible says about discipline: you may not enjoy it or understand it while it's happening, and you may want to cry out, "Give me a break," but in the end it turns out to be for your own good.

As an adult, I can easily understand that my parents had a tremendous amount of wisdom in making sure we were home by a certain time. They understood much better than we that there were temptations to do the wrong things and hang out with the wrong people when you're a kid out on the streets at night. They knew that my brothers and I weren't capable of handling that kind of freedom because we weren't grown up enough to understand that with that freedom comes responsibility.

Dad: Gentle but Tough

I've always admired and respected my father. But that admiration and respect has turned into almost a sense of awe since I've become a father myself. I may not have fully realized it as a kid—at times during my childhood I thought he was downright mean—but my dad was an incredible father in every way.

My brothers and I grew up knowing there was something we could always count on: Dad. He is probably one of the most stable people I've ever known. He's a man you can depend on and trust no matter what the circumstances. He never gets overwhelmed when challenges come, and he never gets overexcited at the good things when they come. (The exception, however, is when he watches me play football!) He was always level-headed and cool, even when the pressure was on. He still is.

My father is probably the most consistent person I've ever known, and that allowed me and my brothers to grow up knowing that Dad would be there for us, no matter how busy he was, no matter how many hours of overtime he had to work, or no matter how tired he was from a long day's work.

Dad would get up every morning between four and five o'clock to head off for work at the Union Carbide plant in New Orleans, a job he held since he graduated from Southern University. After work, he would come straight to the ballpark to see us play or directly home when we weren't playing.

I'm filled with gratitude toward my father for the way he worked so hard to provide for his family and for the way he took such a personal interest in what I was doing. But what I most appreciate about my dad now that I'm a grown man with a wife and a daughter is that he understood the value of discipline. He knew that discipline included some old-fashioned corporal punishment when we messed up, but he also understood the value of giving his boys hugs and pats on the back when we did something well or when we needed encouragement.

Both of my parents were huggers and encouragers when it came to their boys. Mom and Dad showed us much physical affection and told us often that they loved us and were proud of us. I could always talk to both of them when I needed to, and they always had an encouraging word for me when I needed it.

While Dad was an affectionate, compassionate, gentle, loving father, he was also a strict disciplinarian. Some people might think my dad was hard on us. I don't know about that, but I do know this: he was exactly what he needed to be.

My dad just didn't put up with foolishness from his kids. We always knew where we stood with him. Dad's a very straightforward guy, and there was never any doubt what was expected of us. Dad has never been afraid to tell people what he's thinking, and he certainly doesn't fall in line with popular opinion. He would tell his boys what was what, whether or not we wanted to hear it.

Dad has never been the kind of person who can be duped by anybody or anything, especially his kids. We couldn't understand it at the time, but it seemed like we couldn't pull anything over on Dad without him finding out. And believe me, we tried! (My guess is that Dad remembered the kind of tricks he tried to pull when he was a boy.)

Dad was a tough disciplinarian, but he was fair and balanced when it came to correcting us. He drew lines we knew not to step over, but at the same time he wasn't a dictator. That taught us a lot about responsibility and respect for authority.

Dad didn't raise perfect kids—we ultimately had to make our own choices, and we did our share of dirt, even though Dad almost always caught on to us—but we grew up understanding right from wrong. We understood the importance of respecting authority, and we understood the concept of consequences when we bucked that authority.

The Fear of the Father

I remember my father telling me and my brothers, "If you ever get in trouble and have to choose between me and the police, you'd better choose the police." The message behind that was simple enough: facing a night in jail or in juvenile detention was nothing compared with facing an angry father when we got home.

I loved my dad, but there was an element of fear on my part when it came to keeping my nose clean. I wasn't afraid of my father in the way most people understand that word. I didn't feel a sense of dread when I thought of him, at least not when I walked the straight and narrow. I knew that as long as I stayed out of trouble I had nothing to fear, but I also knew that he'd come down on me when I did wrong. I always knew there were consequences for my actions, and that those consequences would come when he found out what I had done.

You may be wondering if I ever got in trouble with my dad. You'd better believe it! I messed up a lot when I was a kid—be it doing what I wasn't supposed to or not doing what I was—and Dad never let it go unpunished when I did. That's another of many areas in which my dad was consistent.

Fortunately for me, though, I learned a lot about the consequences of angering Dad from my older brother Achilles. It wasn't through what he said to me, either, but through what happened to him. I learned a lot about how my dad handled his kids' nonsense by seeing what happened to Achilles when he messed up, which happened often. Achilles had a talent for getting into trouble with Dad, and I paid attention when that happened. I didn't want the same thing to happen to me.

Time to Work

Dad didn't just teach us how to behave; he taught us how to work, not by telling us how as much as showing us how. Dad was a great example to us of the value of working hard for what you get. Every morning when Dad got up at four or five o'clock and headed off to work, he showed us that working was an important part of life.

We first learned how to work at home, where we did all the household chores such as cleaning up the house and washing the dishes. We didn't always enjoy the work, and we often tried to get out of it. I still remember when we asked Dad when he was going to buy a dishwasher. His response? "Why should I buy a dishwasher? I've already got three!" We moaned and groaned about it at the time, but—like everything else my parents did for me when I was a kid—I appreciate the fact that I learned how to take care of business around the house. (My wife appreciates that I learned how to do those things, too!)

Even when I was a little kid, my parents encouraged me to work outside the home to make some money. I was only seven when I started working at my uncle's grocery store. It was regular grocery store work—sweeping the floor, stocking shelves, assisting customers, cleaning up—and it taught me the value of working, and it taught me to respect hard work. And it also made me $7 a week. Not bad for a seven-year-old!

From there, I worked all the way through high school—at a summer day-care center, at a Wendy's, and as a cashier at another local grocery store.

Balancing School and Play

I followed my dad's example of how to work, but I also heeded his words about keeping my grades up.

Bad grades were not an option in my home. Dad and Mom didn't get on us to be straight-A students, but they wanted us to work hard and do the best we could. If our best was an A, that's what our parents wanted to see on the report card. On the other hand, if our best in a particular class was a C-plus, then that was fine too.

Dad never expected me or my brothers to become bookworms who do nothing but study. He encouraged us to do other things like play sports and work. He wanted us to learn the importance of living balanced lives. He encouraged and supported us in our athletic endeavors, but he still regularly checked up on us to see that we were getting our homework done and that our grades were where they needed to be.

One reason Dad concerned himself with our grades was that he and Mom expected us to go to college when we graduated from high school. In fact, there was never a question that Malcolm, Achilles, and I would be going to college.

For me, though, it was a question of where I would go to college and how I would get there.

Football: A Ticket to College?

As I approached the end of my senior year at Alcee Fortier High School, there was no question in my mind or my parents' that I would be going to college. What we didn't know, though, was where I was going and whether it would come through an athletic scholarship or through academics.

Fortunately, I'd worked hard at both school and football.

Sports were always an important part of that balanced life Dad tried to help me and my brothers lead. Dad never pushed us to participate in sports, but he supported us from the time we started playing.

Baseball and football were my sports, and I started playing when I was very young. I started playing Little League baseball when I was seven and Pop Warner football at an even younger age.

I had a lot of success in football at a young age. I played with a group of kids who were dominant in their weight division. We won the city championship at every level, and I played a big part in our success.

By the time our group got to seventh and eighth grade, we had grown bigger and more dominant than ever. I was one of several outstanding players on those teams, and we won our games by an average of more than fifty points. At that time, it looked like I might be ready to move on to a dominating high school career. That didn't happen, though, at least not at first.

When I hit ninth grade, I started struggling with fear on the football field, and I didn't play a lot. I had gone from being a star to a benchwarmer in less than a year! I remember looking at the guys I played against when I got to ninth grade, and I remember thinking how big they looked. It seemed to me that those guys should have been playing on the high school varsity team. For the first time since I started playing football, I was intimidated.

In addition to feeling intimidated, I was faced with playing a new position—cornerback. I hadn't played that position much in youth football, and I was, to say the least, nervous. When I looked at the big, talented athletes I was playing against, I was just afraid of getting beaten. I've always been one to believe in respecting my opponent. But this wasn't respect; it was fear. I was afraid to fail. Of course it hindered my performance.

I didn't have a good ninth-grade year in football, but things would get better for me in high school. After a while, that is.

A Steady Rise

I was a late bloomer as a high school football player. My tenth-grade year also found me, with the exception of some special teams plays, spending most of our games on the bench.

I started my junior season in high school exactly where I had finished my sophomore year—on the bench. I was feeling a little frustration and a lot of envy because several of the guys in my class—some of whom I had played with when we were younger—were playing well and making major contributions to the team. I wanted badly to be out there with them. I couldn't stand being on the bench just watching. My chance soon came, however.

As my junior year wore on, I played more and more in different positions in our defensive backfield, particularly cornerback. (I had given up playing offense by the time I got to high school because I didn't like people running into me all the time.) Although cornerback was the position I eventually played in college and in the NFL, I had a hard time adjusting to it in high school. I think it was tough for me to play the position mostly because I had believed what some coaches had been saying to me as I got older and moved up in the level of play. They had put limitations on me, saying I didn't have the kind of speed or "loose hips" you need to play cornerback. I always respected my coaches, and I think what they said had sunk in, because I went out on the field not really believing I could play the position. Consequently, I frequently got beaten by people I had all the ability I needed to cover.

Although I struggled early in my junior year, I wouldn't quit. Dad had instilled in me the value of perseverance—the attitude that once I started something, I finished it, even when things got tough for me. I stuck with it, and soon I got the chance I had been waiting for.

A Starter—But Where?

One day at practice, the coach approached me and asked me what I thought of playing linebacker for the team. I'd never played the position before, and I didn't think I was big enough to do it. I wanted to play regularly, but I didn't know if I wanted to do it this way. I told him I'd think about it.

I went home and told Dad what the coaches were thinking of doing with me, and he said the same thing I had been thinking: "Colleges aren't going to look at you if you play linebacker. You're not big enough to play that position in college." Dad knew what I was thinking. Even though I was hardly a star in high school football at that point, I still thought I had a chance to play college football some day. I knew and Dad knew that college football isn't often an option for 180-pound high school linebackers.

I went back to practice the next day and told my coach that I'd play linebacker if he really needed me to but that I didn't want to play the position and that I didn't think I'd be very good at it. At that point, I would have played there if the coach had insisted, but he didn't. Instead, they put me in another position: strong safety. It was a position where I thrived throughout the rest of my high school football career.

Although the Alcee Fortier High School team had a down year (we finished around .500—that after a great year when I was a sophomore), I had a good second half of my junior season. I began to grow more and more comfortable playing the strong safety position, and before I knew it I had grown into a confident football player. I was looking forward to what was to be an outstanding senior year, both for me personally and for my team.

We had a great team my senior year at Fortier. We were undefeated in our district before going on to lose a close playoff game to the eventual Louisiana state champion in the state playoffs.

Even though I had started out slowly in my high school football career, I wound up becoming an outstanding player. I had an outstanding senior season and was named the most valuable player in New Orleans and selected for the all-district first team.

What Next?

With my high school career finished, it was time for me to think about where I would be playing college football the following autumn. One problem, though: I wasn't getting recruited. It surprises people to hear it now, but I wasn't getting much, if any, attention from college football programs after I finished my senior year.

One of the assistant coaches at Fortier—Robert Welch, who at that time was the offensive coordinator but has since been promoted to head coach— did all he could to help me and the other seniors on the team. He sent out letters and made phone calls to schools trying to get scholarship offers, but with few results for me.

The only offer I got was an academic scholarship to Dartmouth University. Getting an offer from a school like Dartmouth, a prestigious Ivy League college in Hanover, New Hampshire, was quite an honor for me, but I turned it down.

I wasn't terribly disappointed that I wasn't getting athletic scholarship offers. Sure, if I'd gotten a scholarship offer to a good football school that I was interested in, I'd have snapped it up. But to tell the truth, playing college football wasn't really that important to me. I had other plans anyway.

I didn't think about it much at the time, but I can see now how important Dad's balanced approach to raising me was. It was because of his emphasis on a balanced life that I had another option, an option I really wanted to take.

I was going to enroll at Southern University, where my father had gone to school and where Achilles was currently studying.

PASS COVERAGE

1. Do you have a lot of respect for your mother and father? Why or why not?

2. What role have your parents played in making you the kind of person you are now?

3. Do you see your father as more of a taskmaster or as a loving, kind person? What makes you see him that way?

4. Do you find it difficult making adjustments when things don't go as you planned? Why?

CHAPTER THREE

I'M NOT PLAYING!

PUTTING SCHOOL FIRST AT SOUTHERN

Many are the plans in a man's heart,
but it is the Lord's purpose that prevails.

—PROVERBS 19:21

I had no intention of ever playing organized football again when I arrived at Southern University in Baton Rouge, Louisiana, early in the summer of 1986. I skipped summer vacation after I graduated from Fortier High School and went directly to college. As far as I was concerned, my last football game at Fortier High School was my last game, period. If I played football in college it would be intramural games with my friends.

I've been asked lots of times if I had an itch to play football during those first two years in college. To tell you the truth, not only did I not miss it, I hardly thought about it. I didn't even miss it when I went to the Southern games to see the team play.

I worked hard in class those first two years, and I had a good time, too. I was getting good grades, having fun partying with my friends, and participating in student government, first as a freshman senator, then as the sophomore class vice president.

You might say I was a model student; in fact, I was on pace to graduate with my degree in accounting in three years. From there, my plan was to go out and get a job and start earning a living.

I couldn't see it at the time, but God had other plans, and He used my brother's graduation to slow me down and place me in the center of those plans.

Changing Direction

I lived those first two years of college in an off-campus apartment with Achilles, something I found out was unusual for a freshman. I had pledged to a fraternity, but the thought of living with all those guys never appealed to me. I preferred to stay in my apartment with my brother.

Ever since I can remember, I'd always wanted to be with my big brother Achilles. We were close in age—less than two years apart—and that made for a closeness between us that I didn't have with my oldest brother, Malcolm. From the time I could walk, everywhere Achilles went, I went, and everything he did, I did. I was like his shadow. We played together, worked together, got into trouble together. We were inseparable as kids, then later as college students. We even had the same college major: accounting.

That all changed prior to my junior year at Southern, however.

Just as I had been doing, Achilles had taken the fast track to college graduation. At the end of my sophomore year, he graduated from Southern with his degree in accounting and left me on my own.

As it turns out, his graduating was the best thing that could have happened to me. Suddenly, I wasn't just "Achilles's little brother" to the people at Southern who knew me. It was like I had instantly become my own person. I'd been patterning my college life after Achilles's, but with him gone I realized I had the rest of my life to work and that there was no reason for me to rush through the college experience. I still studied hard, but I slowed down a little and began enjoying school more than I had.

As it turns out, God slowed me down just enough to get me moving in the direction He wanted me to go: back to the football field.

"You Should Play, Aeneas!"

When God wants you to do something He has a wonderful way of shifting circumstances and people around to move you and motivate you.

I was completely content just being a student during my first two years in college, but there was a seed being planted in my heart, a seed that would one day grow into a new desire in my heart to play college football.

It didn't happen right away, though. As hard as it may be for some people to believe, I resisted the idea of playing football, even though people I knew were trying to encourage me to go out.

I played some intramural football with my friends during my freshman and sophomore years, and I played pretty well. I'd kept myself in shape and I could still run pretty well, even though I hadn't been involved in any serious athletic competition.

Some of the guys I played with were members of the Southern University football team, and a couple of them suggested that I come out for football. One player in particular—Michael Lindsey, a nose guard for the Jaguars and a former teammate of mine at Fortier High School—seemed to make it his personal goal in life to persuade me to come out for the team.

Every time I saw Michael—whether it was in class, at the cafeteria, at a party, or at a campus event—he'd say the same thing: "Man, you should come out for football. You're still a player, and I think you could help the team."

While I appreciated Michael's confidence in my ability, I still wasn't interested in playing, so just to get him off my back, I told him I'd think about it. And I did think about it, but never seriously. I just didn't want to play.

There was also a member of my family who wanted me to play. No, it wasn't my dad. It would have been fine with him, but he was happy just to see me working hard and getting good grades and participating in student government. It was my uncle, William Woodson, who at every family gathering would practically beg me to play college football. "Why aren't you playing football, Nicky?" he'd ask, using his nickname for me. "You should be playing."

I wasn't ready to tell Michael Lindsey or my uncle—or the Southern University coach, for that matter—that I'd decided to go out for football the following season, but as time went on I was definitely considering it. Looking back I'm reminded of the Bible's account of Mary after Jesus' birth. In Luke 2:19 it says, "Mary treasured up all these things and pondered them in her heart." That's exactly what I did. I pondered it over in my heart and considered what I was going to do. Finally, I made a decision.

Football Weather

Anybody who's ever played football or been a football fan knows what the term "football weather" means. It starts in September when it's still warm out but starting to cool. You can feel the change in the weather. You feel the breeze and the cooling temperatures and you smell the fresh-cut grass. You know it's time for football!

That's exactly what I was thinking one early September day in 1988 as I left the Southern University library. It was the week before the first game of the season—the team had already been practicing for several weeks—and I suddenly became aware that it was time for football.

It had been really warm earlier in the day, but a front came through and it was cool outside. *Man, this is football weather,* I thought, and I started to feel nostalgic, thinking about how much I enjoyed playing high school football. It hit me all at once: I actually missed playing football! I was feeling an itch I hadn't felt for the previous two years. I really *wanted* to play.

Just then, in an incident that I know now was divinely orchestrated, my friend Michael Lindsey appeared. He was on his way from football practice to the cafeteria for supper. He spotted me and stopped and smiled at me. Then came the question that had become almost a personal ritual between us, like two friends greeting one another with their own personal handshake that no one else knows about: "Why don't you come out for football?" This time, though, there was more seriousness in his voice, as if to say, "You can still play *this season* if you come out *right away.*"

I looked at Michael and without hesitation, I said, "I will. I'll be at practice tomorrow." I had told Michael many times that I would think about it or that I'd do it the following season, so he might have thought that I was just brushing him off again. But I meant it this time. I was going out for the Southern University football team.

I Want to Play, Coach!

I walked into Coach Percy Duhé's office the day after my meeting with
Michael Lindsey and informed him that I wanted to come out for football—
that day! I don't remember how he looked at me or what he said, and I don't
know if he took me very seriously, but he gave me the name of the team's
equipment manager and told me where to go to get started.

I don't know if the equipment manager thought I was just going to be
practice fodder for the varsity, or if he didn't think I was serious about playing football, but he issued me what might be the worst practice gear ever
worn by a college football player. It was what is commonly known in college
football circles as "suicide equipment," and it included a helmet that didn't fit
right, shoulder pads with parts missing, and torn and stained pants and jer-
sey. I'm sure I didn't look like much in that gear, but I didn't care about that. I
couldn't wait to get out on the field to see how well I lined up with guys who
had been playing college football while I studied and partied the previous
two years.

I'll never forget my first day of practice. In one respect, I felt like a little
kid out there, running around and playing with all the enthusiasm I'd had
when I played youth football. It was like I'd found a new love for the game.
On the other hand, it was like I'd never left the game because I was out there
covering guys and making plays like a veteran. From that first day in practice, I felt like I belonged.

The next step for me, though, was to achieve my goal of making the
team. To do that, I was going to have to impress Coach Marino Casem who
was a carbon copy of my father, only turned up a couple of notches. Coach
Casem is still one of the toughest coaches I've ever played for. A no-nonsense,
old-fashioned kind of coach, he would push his players to their limits and
beyond. He was tough!

Like my dad, Coach Casem knew the value of hard work. I might not
have thought about it much at the time, but Coach Casem was going to continue a process in me that my dad had started as I was growing up.

Play Me Some Travelin' Music

I didn't start out my college football career with grandiose plans of one day playing in the National Football League. I wasn't even interested in whether I was all-conference or all-American. In fact, starting wasn't even on my mind at the time. I had one simple goal: making the traveling squad. When you make the traveling squad in college football, you've truly made the team. There are guys who dress for home games (Have you ever seen a home University of Nebraska game televised? It looks like they're sending a small army out there!) but don't travel with the team to away games. I didn't want to be one of those guys.

Because I'd only been practicing for a week, I knew I wouldn't be playing in our first game. But I was going to do my best to make the trip to Houston, Texas, for the team's second game of the season against Texas Southern.

That was my goal, and I was going to make sure there wasn't anything I didn't do to help make that goal a reality. All I could think those first two weeks of practice was, *Man, I've got to make the traveling team!*

We opened the season with a home game against Alabama State. I wanted to get out there in the worst way, but I understood from the beginning that I wouldn't be playing. My sights were set on another goal.

I knew making the traveling team as a player on the regular defense was going to be a long shot—maybe too long. But I also knew that there was a place for me to get my foot in the door: special teams. I gave my all at every practice, hoping to catch the eye of the Southern University coaching staff. I played every special teams play like my college football career depended on it. I listened to the coaches and did everything they told me, exactly the way they told me. Still, I didn't know. At least not until late that week after practice.

The Southern University coaching staff had posted the list of who would be making the trip to Houston in the locker room. With a mixture of apprehension and excitement, I walked up to the list and looked for my name. Suddenly I realized that all my hard work had paid off. I would be traveling with my new team that Saturday for our game against Texas Southern!

Breaking the Good News

I couldn't wait to tell someone that I'd made the Southern University traveling squad. Breaking the news was going to be all the more fun because I hadn't told anyone that I had gone out for the team. I had decided from the beginning that I was going to keep this to myself, at least until I knew I'd made it.

Dad followed the Southern University football team in the papers, and he went to a few games. I had a feeling he might want to be at this one. I called my parents from my apartment.

When I got Dad on the phone, I asked him, "Are you and Mom going to the game at Texas Southern this Saturday?" I knew they had no plans to go, but I couldn't resist setting up some suspense.

"Why would we go to the Texas Southern game?" he said. "No, we hadn't planned on it."

"Are you sure you don't want to come and see your son play?" I asked.

Dad got quiet for a moment, then asked "What are you talking about?"

"I walked on and I'm playing on the team," I finally told him. "I've made the traveling squad, and we're going to Texas Southern this Saturday. Well, do you want to come?"

By this time, I think Dad thought I was teasing him. He had no idea that I was even interested in playing football at Southern, let alone that I had actually gone out for the team. It took awhile before I was sure that he believed me. Eventually, though, I persuaded him and Mom to come to the game.

I did a similar set up with my buddies at college. Like Mom and Dad, they had no idea what I'd been doing the previous two weeks, and that made for some fun for me when I told them.

There was a group of us talking in a dorm room a few days before the Texas Southern game, and the subject of traveling to Houston came up. We'd made it our personal tradition to travel to all the away games, and this one was not going to be an exception. The only difference was, I wouldn't be traveling with my friends.

They were talking about going to Houston, and somebody turned to me and asked if I was planning on going. "Yeah," I said. "I'm going, but not with you guys."

It was almost unthinkable! What was I saying? How could I break our tradition like that?

"What do you mean you're not going with us?" one of my friends asked. "Who else would you go with?"

"I'm going with the team."

"What do you mean you're going with the team? Do you work with the team?"

"No, I'm on the team. I'm playing. I'm traveling with the team this week."

I knew then that my friends didn't believe me, that they thought this was some kind of joke. To this day, I doubt if they believed me, at least until they saw me on the field with my teammates.

On My Way Up

Southern University's football team plays in the NCAA Division 1-AA Southwestern Athletic Conference, which also includes schools such as Prairie View A & M, Alcorn State, Alabama State, and Grambling State, which was coached at the time I played by the legendary Eddie Robinson, the all-time winningest coach in college football history.

It's extremely unlikely that you'll see Southern—or any other Southwestern Athletic Conference team for that matter—in the lead story on ESPN's *SportsCenter* or on the front page of any of the major sports magazines. It's a relatively small school in that it competes at the NCAA Division 1-AA level, which is one level lower than what football fans would usually consider the "big boys." As a Division 1-AA school, Southern doesn't play against Division 1-A national powers such as Florida, Florida State, Tennessee, or even Louisiana State located in the same city as Southern.

The day I played my first college football game, there wasn't much national attention on my team or the team we were playing. In the bigger picture of collegiate sports, it just wasn't all that important.

I couldn't have possibly cared less about that, though. All I cared about was that I was on the field with my teammates—wearing a nice uniform this time—for our game with Texas Southern and that my mother and father and friends were somewhere in the stands to help me enjoy this special day.

I played on the special teams, and I couldn't believe how good it felt to be on the field. I don't remember how many tackles I made—if I made any— but I had a great time. It was a good time for the Jaguars, too, as we won 24-16 to go 2-0 on the season. (We'd beaten Alabama State the previous week.)

It's hard to explain how I felt. It was almost like a dream. I remember Dad coming down on the field after the game and giving me one of those hugs that you *knew* you'd been hugged when it was done. I can't remember if Dad said anything—I think he was like me, just soaking everything in—but I remember a look on his face that let me know how proud he was that his boy was a part of the Southern University football team.

I was feeling pretty good about myself. Just two weeks into the season I'd achieved the goal I'd set when I went out for football. But now it was time to set some higher goals. I hadn't played on snap on the Jaguars' regular defense when in Houston, and I wanted a chance to do just that. It was time to get back to work.

Taking the Next Step

I continued to work hard in practice the following week. I did everything the coaches told me to do and gave it everything I could on every play. And all the hard work paid off, too, as I was given some playing time on the regular defense over the next couple of weeks. I played and made six tackles the following week against Prairie View A & M (unfortunately, we lost 20-14), then made a couple of tackles in a 45-7 win over Mississippi Valley State. I had five tackles, a fumble recovery, and a sack in my fourth game, a 23-3 loss to Jackson State.

I was really starting to get my coaches' attention during those four weeks, and it was about to pay off big-time as I was moved into the starting lineup for our game at Alcorn State. I got a break that week when one of the defensive starters got in some trouble with the coaches, and I was ready when I got the call.

I played what is commonly referred to in football as a "rover" in my first start. It was kind of a hybrid linebacker/defensive back, and it put me in position to be around the ball and make plays. I made some plays too, including two quarterback sacks and my first interception in a college game. I can still remember how much fun it was to be out there running around and doing all I could to help my team win. I also remember that we lost, unfortunately to Alcorn State 27-7, our third straight defeat.

I was playing well and having a great time during my first year of college football, but the team went into a midseason funk, losing four in a row at one point to go 3–5. We knew we'd have to win our remaining three games to finish with a winning record, and that wasn't going to be easy, because our season-ending game was against a very strong Grambling State team.

We beat Bethune-Cookman 20-13 and I had my second interception of the season to go with nine tackles. Then we beat Tennessee State 10-7 to go 5-5 and set up our season-ending matchup with Grambling State, which had an 8-2 record going into the game.

The game with Grambling was big for us, not only because it gave us a chance to have a winning season, but because it was in what had become the biggest game of the year for black colleges: the annual Bayou Classic at the Superdome in New Orleans.

My first Bayou Classic was unforgettable.

Going Big-Time

The Bayou Classic is like the Rose Bowl for black colleges, and it's become quite an event for the Big Easy. There is an air of festivity in New Orleans during the week leading up to the Bayou Classic. There are parties, rallies, pageants, and any number of community events culminating with the biggest game on the Southern University and Grambling State football schedules. As one former Southern University coach once put it, "It's like Mardi Gras and New Year's Eve rolled into one."

Not only do 70,000 loyal fans from all over the country show up at the Superdome, but hundreds of thousands more watch the game on what has become an annual television event. Not bad for a couple of Division 1-AA schools!

The Bayou Classic was the brainchild of Grambling State Coach Eddie Robinson, who had envisioned a game that would become an annual tradition for black college football; a splashy, season-ending extravaganza featuring a game between the same two bitter rivals every season: Grambling State and Southern.

This game is huge for the players and coaches at both schools. It's Division 1-AA's version of Army-Navy, USC-UCLA, Florida-Florida State, or Ohio State-Michigan.

Neither program needs all the Bayou Classic hype to get themselves ready for the game. Both teams know that winning the game can make or break their season. I didn't need all the noise to get my attention either, and I didn't need the fact that I was playing against a legendary coach to get me ready to play. To tell you the truth, I didn't think much about all the hoopla or about Coach Robinson. I already had plenty to think about going into that game. I had just been moved to the cornerback position, and I and my teammates on the Southern defense were about to take on the league's top offense.

Led by All-SWAC quarterback Clemente Gordon, the Tigers had put up some huge numbers on offense. To top things off, they were looking for some payback that week because Southern had beaten them the season before, ending the school's string of twenty-seven straight winning seasons.

We had been playing pretty well on defense the previous two weeks, but we knew that if we didn't come out ready to play, the Tigers would run us out of the Superdome in a hurry. I couldn't wait for the challenge. Finally, the day came for my first Classic.

I remember going out on the Superdome field. I had looked forward to this day, but when it finally came, it was beyond anything I could have imagined. I'd played in the Superdome before—when I was in high school—but that was nothing like this. It's impossible for me to put into words the feelings I had as I ran out onto that field with the roar of the sellout crowd ringing in my ears. I felt that rush of adrenaline.

It was game time!

We were the big underdogs. Most people thought we'd get our share of points but that the Grambling State offense would overwhelm us. That didn't happen though. In fact, we did something no other team had come close to doing that season: we kept Grambling State out of the end zone. We won 10-3 to secure not only our winning season, but bragging rights in the state of Louisiana for one year. Me, I had a memorable game racking up a season-high eleven tackles from my cornerback spot.

Beating Grambling was the perfect ending to a season that turned out to be something greater than I'd ever dreamed of. Although I didn't realize it at the time, I truly believe that I had God's favor in my life that year. In His perfect timing, He placed in me a desire to play football, and after I went out for the team, He made a way for me to earn favor with the Southern University coaches.

My first year with the Southern University football team was a great time for me, and I continued to build on a good thing my second year.

I had only just begun!

Getting Started On Time

There was no question in my mind during the summer of 1989 what I would be doing later that year: I was heading back to Baton Rouge to join my team to prepare for the upcoming football season. After what had happened during my first year with the team, I couldn't wait to get back at it.

There was a feeling of optimism among the players heading into the 1989 season. We had won our last three games in 1988 to finish with a winning season, and we were returning a good group of players from that team. What we weren't returning, though, was Coach Marino Casem, who stepped down as coach of the Jaguars after my first year. His successor was Gerald

Kimble, a first-year college coach whose style was the exact opposite of Coach Casem's. While Coach Casem was something of a taskmaster, Coach Kimble had a more subdued, laid-back style.

Some people wondered how we'd respond to such a different coaching style. Pretty well, as it turned out.

We started out strong in 1989, going 5-1, with our only loss in those first six games coming from Texas Southern, a team that had gone 0-11 the previous season. I had a good first six games, recording thirty-four tackles and four interceptions. Unfortunately, we struggled a little bit over our next four games, going 1-2-1, with our only win over that stretch a 31-28 victory over Nicholls State.

That left us with a 6-3-1 record heading into our season-ending game with Grambling. The Tigers had a lot riding on the game: a win would give them a 7-0 record in the SWAC and the undisputed conference championship.

The Tigers were again an impressive offensive team. They were huge up front and had all-conference quarterback Clemente Gordon and a future All-Pro-caliber receiver by the name of Jake Reed. (Jake now plays for the Minnesota Vikings.)

My second Bayou Classic was everything the first one wasn't. Instead of a low-scoring defensive battle that we won, it was an offensive shootout that Grambling State won 44-30. I had a big game with eleven tackles and an interception, but it still hurt to lose. We felt as low after losing in 1989 as we felt high after winning in 1988. It was a crushing defeat for us, and we all knew we'd have to wait a year for a chance at redemption.

The loss to Grambling notwithstanding, we had a pretty good season, finishing 6-4-1 overall and 4-3 in the SWAC.

Personally, I had a great season, with eighty-four tackles and seven interceptions, which was second in the nation that year. I was named first-team All-Southwestern Athletic Conference and Black College All-America.

By the way, there was one other honor that was being talked about during that time.

A Pro Prospect

It felt good to receive the personal recognition for my play, but there was one other development for me that season: there was serious talk that I could be headed to the NFL after my college career was through.

As far as I know, it started around the time of our game with Jackson State. I had a big game, including a fifty-seven-yard interception return for what turned out to be the game-winning touchdown. It just so happened that the game was televised, and Lem Barney—himself a Hall of Fame cornerback with the Detroit Lions—was the color commentator. After the game, Lem introduced himself to me and my parents and told them that I would one day be playing in the NFL.

I hadn't given playing professional football any serious thought before then. Frankly, I just didn't think I was good enough to play at that level. But here was Lem Barney saying with seriousness and conviction that I was going to play in the NFL.

That kind of talk continued throughout the latter part of my junior year. After awhile, it became clear: I was definitely being looked at as an NFL prospect.

But before I would get started on my road to the NFL, God had to show me some things about submission. And it started with me giving everything I had to Him.

PASS COVERAGE

1. Can you remember a time when you were content in what you were doing, only to have God change your plans for you? How did you respond?

2. What are some of the ways God has prompted you to change direction in your life?

3. How do you respond to unexpected success in your life?

4. How do you respond when people say good things about you or about your accomplishments?

CHAPTER FOUR

SUBMITTING MYSELF TO JESUS CHRIST

Jesus said to his disciples, "If anyone would come after me,
he must deny himself and take up his cross and follow me."
—MATTHEW 16:24

If you were to ask most people about it, I imagine you would find that just about everybody has had a time in his or her life when there were big changes. I'm talking about the kind of changes that alter the entire course of a person's life.

I had a season like that myself.

The spring and summer of 1990 was a time when I went through the most radical changes of my life—both as a football player and as a person. It was a time when God brought people and events into my life that would change not just my future as a football player, but my whole eternity.

I was coming off a strong junior season at Southern, a season in which I began hearing a lot of talk about how I was an NFL prospect. Looking back on that time in my life, though, I can see that I wasn't ready to think about playing professional football.

God got me ready, though, first by bringing a man into my life who helped make me the football player I would become.

Learning to Fly

Brian Thomas, one of my teammates at Southern University, was a track man who happened to play wide receiver on the football team, and he was one of the fastest men I've ever known. Even after my years in the NFL I'm still amazed when I think about how fast he was. He could run by people like they were standing still, and I'm not talking about slow people, either. Brian routinely ran the 40-yard-dash in 4.3 seconds.

Brian wasn't the kind of guy you could walk up to and make friends with easily. He was a quiet guy who kept to himself most of the time. But I had to talk to him. I had to ask him how he ran as fast as he did. One day, after the football season ended, I approached him and asked a simple question: "Brian, how do you run that fast?"

Then, with one of those "you should know this" looks on his face, Brian looked at me and said, "You could run a 4.3."

I looked at him in amazement. I couldn't believe he was serious, but he said it with such confidence that he looked like he would have bet every cent he had on it. Obviously, he saw something in me that I couldn't see in myself.

"Me? Running a 4.3?" I asked.

"Yeah, with some work, you can run a 4.3," he said. "Right now, you just don't know how to run."

Brian talked to me about his training, and it got me to thinking. I wondered, *Just how fast could I run?* Even though the scouts were looking at me, I wasn't considered that fast by NFL standards. I'd run in the 4.5–4.6 range in the 40, which is probably slightly below average for an NFL cornerback.

I started to think that going out for track would help my speed as a football player. At that point, I decided that I would do it: I would go out for the Southern University track team that spring, and I would ask Brian if he would work out with me in preparation.

I knew that Brian could teach me some things about speed. I saw Brian shortly before the Christmas break. "I want to run track this spring and I want to work out with you to get ready. I want to learn to run faster and I want to see what you do to run that fast," I told him.

Brian agreed to work out with me, but at the same time warned me that I'd have hard work to do in order to reach my potential.

At that moment, I decided that I was going to submit myself to Brian and do whatever he told me to do when we worked out. Brian wasn't an authority figure in the same way a parent, a teacher, or a coach is, but in my mind he was an authority figure. Why? Because he knew something I didn't know and had something I didn't have. I knew that if I was going to reach my potential, I was going to have to do what he told me to do when he told me to do it and with all the effort I could muster.

I went home to New Orleans with Brian that Christmas break, and while everybody else was home relaxing, eating, and celebrating the holiday, we worked out. Let me tell you, that was some of the hardest work I've ever done in my life.

Time to Train

It didn't take me long to realize that Brian was absolutely right about me not knowing how to run. Sure, I was an All-American on the football field, and I had relatively good speed—good enough that I was being touted as a potential NFL player—but I hadn't come close to my potential simply because I didn't know how to get the most out of my body. Brian, on the other hand, knew about those things.

Brian was so fast that all I could do was follow him. I couldn't keep up with him. As hard as I ran, he still blew by me like I was a statue. I did my best to stay with him through hours and hours of training. I tried to do everything he did the same way he did it. In each session, we'd run a 100, a 200, a 300, a 400, a 600, then an 800, and then we'd reverse the order of the sprints and run some more. After that, we'd go run up and down the stands at the stadium where we worked out. Then we'd stretch out.

I couldn't believe how much my body hurt. A couple of times I wondered if I would survive the punishment I was putting myself through. All that time, Brian pushed me to keep running. At times, I'd lay on the ground—exhausted, panting, getting sick to my stomach, and feeling almost unbearable pain—and Brian would look at me and say, "Let's go!" He wouldn't let me quit.

As miserable as I was during this self-inflicted torture, I wouldn't quit. I had started something, and I intended to finish it. I had learned at an early age that putting yourself in a position to accomplish something often requires endurance, and I was going to endure the training Brian put me through, even if it killed me.

It hurt physically to be submitted to Brian's authority, but I understood that what I was going through was going to be good for me. I did everything he told me to do, even though there were many days when I had to battle my flesh and drag myself to the track. It didn't take long, though, before I started reaping the benefits of our workouts. It was like my body was undergoing a metamorphosis, and I started running faster than I ever dreamed possible.

That spring I went out for track and had a great season. I was the number two sprinter on the Southern University team's depth chart. Although I won some sprints and some relays, I wasn't all-American or a conference champion but that didn't matter to me. What did matter was that I was able to do something I hadn't previously believed I was capable of doing.

Scout Day

After track season I continued to train, and that fall I ran a 4.3 40 in football practice when NFL scouts were present. It was "Scout Day" at Southern University. There were NFL scouts from almost every team there. My time in the 40 changed how I was perceived by the NFL. I was no longer a prospect with potential but now a possible first-round draft pick.

I praise God for bringing Brian Thomas into my life at just the right time and for giving me enough smarts to submit myself to Brian and to learn from him some things I would need later to become successful in the National Football League.

I still believe that God saw something in me that I couldn't see in myself at that time and that He used another person—a person with whom I developed a friendship and for whom I still feel a deep sense of gratitude—to bring out in me what had up to that point been hidden.

God was far from finished with bringing out the hidden things in me, though. During the months after I started working out with Brian, there would be changes in my life that would alter where I was headed, not just in my career, but for eternity.

A Taste of the NFL—And Much More

After that track season in the spring of 1990 I headed home to New Orleans and immediately set about getting myself ready for the following football season. I worked out with some friends from the New Orleans area who would be playing in the NFL that season: Maurice Hurst (New England Patriots), Clarence Verdin (Indianapolis Colts), and Kevin Lewis (San Francisco 49ers).

It was a great experience to work out with players who had NFL experience, and I did everything I could to learn from those guys. I learned about footwork and technique, and I also got a feel for what it was like to work out with players of that caliber.

I knew that what I had learned that summer would help me in the coming months. But there was one other thing I got out of that summer: it was my new relationship with the Lord Jesus Christ.

I was a typical college jock. I drank, I partied, I played around, I lied, I stole. In short, I was a sinner who didn't even know he needed to be saved.

Even though I'd gone to church when I was a kid, I still had no point of reference for God or what His existence had to do with me. All I could remember about church, really, was that I'd gone. I couldn't remember the teaching, the preaching, or anything else about church. I barely remembered what the place looked like.

So I had the advantage of not having any preconceived biases or notions about Christianity. I had no mental strongholds or rationalizations about what Jesus Christ had to do with me. My only knowledge about God was that there was one. Other than that, I had no idea what God's existence had to do with me.

I was about to find out.

Two Pictures of Christ

It's been said about us Christians that we may be the only picture of Jesus some people will ever see in this world. I, for one, am grateful for that, because it was through two pictures of Jesus I knew in college that I came to a point of knowing I needed Jesus Christ as my personal Lord and Savior.

I saw that picture first in Kevin Lewis who had played football with me at Fortier High School before going on to Northwestern State in Louisiana. I had always admired Kevin both as a person and as a football player. Kevin was driven and motivated to be the best he could be, but at the same time he had a sense of inner peace that was evident to all who knew him. Kevin also had a way of letting people know that he wasn't going to be influenced to do things he knew were wrong.

While Kevin Lewis was a big influence on me during that time in my life, an even bigger influence was my girlfriend and future wife, Tracy. I met Tracy through a friend of mine who dated her twin sister. (You guessed it, her twin sister's name is Stacy, and they look and act a great deal alike.) I could see from the moment I met her that there was something different about her. Tracy Smith was like no other woman I'd ever met.

The most obvious difference was the way she lived. She associated with a lot of the same people I did, but she didn't drink and party like everybody else I knew at Southern. I also found out from talking to her early in our relationship that she was a virgin and intended to stay one until she got married. I'd always heard of girls like that, and I figured they were around, but Tracy was the first woman with those qualities I'd taken an interest in. Tracy's lifestyle not only intrigued me, it sparked in me an interest to know her better, to find out what she was about and why she lived the kind of life she did.

While I deeply respected Tracy for her lifestyle, I could also see in her that same peace and assurance that I saw in Kevin. I couldn't understand it, but I could see it in how she related to other people, and I could see it up close in how she related to me. We were dating, and I knew that she liked me, but I could also see that she wasn't about to make me the center of her world. That spot, it turns out, was already occupied.

I couldn't put my finger on what I saw in her that intrigued me so much, but I knew Tracy had something I didn't have. I wanted to know what it was.

Neither Tracy nor Kevin preached at me that much during my junior year in college. They both knew I wasn't living the kind of life they were, but

I never felt like they were pointing fingers or condemning me. Yes, they talked to me about their beliefs; in fact, Kevin even took me to Bible study at New Hope Baptist Church in New Orleans when I had a chance to go.

I admired both Tracy and Kevin as much as anybody I knew at the time, and I found myself admiring the other Christian people I was meeting. I admired the fact that they didn't mind being different from most of the students at Southern. I admired their principles and their sense of right and wrong. I admired that they were submitted to something—someone—when most of the people we knew wanted only to please themselves. Most of all, I admired the sense of peace I could see in them.

As I got to know Tracy and Kevin better, I found myself wanting very badly to have what they had.

Submitting to God

I didn't fully understand it then, but during that summer of 1990—the summer between my junior and senior football seasons at Southern—I had an appointment with God, an appointment He was going to make sure I kept.

One of the first things I did when I got home for summer vacation that year was open up the phone book and look for a particular church. I didn't know why I was looking for this particular church, only that it had come to my mind when I got home from Baton Rouge.

I'd never been one to put a lot of stock in the idea of God speaking directly to someone and directing them to a place He wanted them to go. Since then, though, I've come to the point where I believe God planted in my mind the name of that church. I knew the church existed, but I didn't know where it was, and I didn't know anybody who attended. I'm not even sure if I knew the name of it. But I opened the phone book and found it: Greater St. Stephen Full Gospel Baptist Church. It was located in uptown New Orleans, just down the street from the junior high school I had attended, Carter G. Woodson Junior High.

When I saw the name of the church in the phone book, I knew with all certainty where I was going to be that Sunday morning. I really had no choice. I didn't know exactly what was going to happen that Sunday, only that I needed to be in church.

Without telling anybody in my family, I got up on that Sunday morning and headed off for church. There was nobody there I knew when I got to Greater St. Stephen's, and that might have been for the better anyway. God wanted my undivided attention. I sat there listening as Bishop Paul S. Morton Sr., the pastor, laid out the gospel in his sermon.

I don't remember exactly what Bishop Morton said, but I do remember for the first time in my life I understood the gospel of Jesus Christ. It was as if blinders had been lifted from my eyes, allowing me to see real truth. The Word of God came alive for me, and I understood that there is a God and that the God who revealed Himself in the Bible loved me so much that He sent His Son Jesus Christ to die on the cross to pay for every rotten thing I had ever done. He had done that—*for me!*

As I sat there, everything inside me was crying out, "This is for you! This is what you've been looking for! This is what Kevin and Tracy have been talking about!" As Bishop Morton finished his sermon, he gave the invitation. The exact words he used escape me, but they went something like this: "I'd like to invite those of you who want to accept Christ to come forward and let me pray with you."

Did he say, "Right now," or "Today"? I don't remember if he did, but it wouldn't have mattered to me if he had, because that's what I desperately wanted to do. The problem was, that old enemy—fear—poked its head inside the church that morning and said to me, *It can wait, Aeneas. Just stay seated. You don't want everybody watching you, anyway. Besides, this is a scary decision, and you don't know what will be required of you. Maybe you'd better think about this some more.*

My heart was pounding and my mouth went dry. Where only a few moments earlier I had thought only about my need for Jesus Christ, now I was thinking about things like what my family would say or how I was all alone that day or how scared I was of what God would ask me to do if I submitted my life to Him. I was afraid of the unknown. Everything inside me was pushing me to go forward, but I didn't go. I was too afraid.

I went home from church still not knowing Jesus Christ in a personal way.

A Temporary Delay

When I think about the week that followed my first visit to Greater St. Stephen, I imagine the devil must have been feeling pretty good about himself. Here I was, as ready as anybody to walk to that altar, bend my knees, and give myself to the Lord, and he scared me out of it. He made me focus on my fears instead of God's love for me. He made me focus on what I didn't know instead of what I did know: that I needed to get saved.

Maybe the devil won a little battle that week, but the ultimate victory was the Lord's. All that week, I said to myself, *I'm going forward this Sunday and I'm going to get saved. Nothing's going to stop me!* I wanted a relationship with Jesus Christ, and I was determined that nothing was going to keep me from my appointment with God.

I'll never forget finally taking that step and submitting myself to God. I had on gray pants and a blue jacket. I didn't look flashy but just like someone who had an important appointment with an extremely important person. (That, in fact, is exactly what I had!)

Like he had the previous week, Bishop Morton gave an invitation for those who wanted to get saved to come forward. I felt a little of the fear I had the week before, but it wasn't going to stop me this time. I rose from my seat, walked down to aisle to the altar, and asked Jesus Christ to be my Lord and Savior.

I didn't have what a lot of people would consider a very "spectacular" salvation experience. I didn't fall on my back and start speaking in tongues, and I didn't break out in tears. God does those things in some people's lives, but that wasn't His plan for me. I remember at that moment I had an incredible sense of peace—a peace I'd never known—flooding my whole being. I knew beyond any doubt that I was in right standing with this God I had ignored my whole life. I knew I was saved forever, and I knew that there was no turning back, that from now on things in my life were going to be different.

They were, too. I no longer had a desire to live the way I had before. I no longer wanted to do anything that I knew was displeasing to God. All I wanted to do was live a life completely submitted to Him and make Him number one in everything I did.

I became like a dry sponge when it came to the Word of God. I soaked up everything I could. I was in church four days a week. If the doors to the church were open and the Word of God was being taught, I was there. I went to church on Tuesdays, Wednesdays, Fridays, and Sundays, and I'd have gone the other three days of the week if it had been open. I couldn't get enough of the fellowship and teaching I was receiving. I just wanted to be around the Word and around people who believed what I now did. It was like I had spent my whole life starving, then found a place where they served the best food you would ever want to eat.

I needed the Word, too, as I was about to embark on a time of incredible testing in my life.

Getting Used to Change

With the change that was taking place in my life, my family and friends started to worry about me. Where before I had shown little or no interest in God, now I was in church four days a week. The way I talked, the way I acted, the things I was interested in—all that changed in a matter of a week. Now the people who knew me wondered if I had fallen under the influence of some kind of cult.

I can understand why people might have been concerned about me. When you see someone change that radically in that short of a time, you naturally wonder what's up. I also think there's a tendency when you don't fully understand something to fear it.

My parents, who hadn't committed their lives to Christ at the time, were concerned, and I think I understand what they were thinking. Mom and Dad had been around long enough to have seen some pretty bizarre things in the news concerning religion. When they saw that their son had become "religious," they immediately thought of the bad things they had seen.

While Mom and Dad had a lot of questions about my newfound faith, they were still as supportive as they knew how to be under the circumstances. They even came to church with me two weeks after I accepted Christ to be there for my baptism. I hadn't intended to tell them about it, but I had to say something when Mom asked me why I needed a white sheet when I asked her for one. (I *was* going to bring it back!) When I explained to her that we needed a white sheet to wrap ourselves in for the baptism, she looked at me and said, "Why didn't you tell us?!"

Not only did Mom and Dad come to see their son baptized, they seemed happy and proud to be there for me. As I've said before, that's just the kind of Mom and Dad I have.

While it was difficult for me to bring my new faith home to Mom and Dad, it was even harder to take it back to school in Baton Rouge.

Back to School

One of the hardest things I've ever had to do was make a stand for Jesus Christ when I returned to Southern in the fall of 1990. I was going back to a place where I had friends who were still living the way I had before: lying, cheating, stealing, drinking, cussing, fornicating.

Now my friends were going to see a new Aeneas. I had changed, and I wasn't going to be doing the same things I had before when I got back to school. It was tough to make that stand, and I felt the same fear I had felt that day I first visited Greater St. Stephen's. But I knew I couldn't back down.

I soon realized that it's okay in the eyes of the world to go to church and express belief in God, but it's another thing to let that belief in God change the way you talk, think, and live. That's when people start thinking you're some kind of radical religious fanatic.

It amazed me how the devil tried to use my friends to get me to go back to the way I'd lived before. I heard every argument you could imagine from friends who thought I'd taken this Jesus stuff too far:

"That might be great for you, but I don't need to hear about it."

"I've been a Christian all my life and I'm doing all right."

"Aeneas, you need to lighten up. You're getting too serious about this religious stuff."

I couldn't back down, though. This was make-or-break time for me, and I had to continue to stand firm.

Taking a Stand

I knew my friends were watching me for any sign of hypocrisy. They wanted to know if this change was real, or if I'd go back to the old life just as soon as the pressures came. Finally a moment of truth time came for me and my declaration of faith.

I went out shopping at Macy's, a nice clothing store in Baton Rouge, with some of my friends. One of them knew a young woman who worked at the store. Before we'd left to go to Macy's, my friend told us, "My friend is going to get us all a big discount on anything we want to buy."

There are times when getting a discount on goods through someone you know is okay. This, however, was not one of those times. This was dishonest and wrong. It was, in a word, stealing.

I picked out some nice, new clothes—stuff I couldn't wait to wear. I tried on everything I wanted to "purchase" at the store, and I looked good! These were beautiful clothes, and expensive, too. Ordinarily, there was no way I could afford clothes like these. This was going to be some deal!

We got home and started to look at the spoils of our trip. Then one of my friends—a guy I'd known since I was a kid and one of my coconspirators that day—looked at me and said, "How could a Christian do something like this? What do you think the Bible says about this?"

At that moment, the words "Thou shalt not steal" rang out in my mind. I knew I had messed up. I had done one of the very things I said I'd never do again. My friend had me where he wanted me. He had caught me in a moment of dishonesty, and he wasn't going to let me get away with it.

There is nothing that hurts worse in the life of a Christian than having a nonbeliever call you out on the carpet when your actions fall short of God's standard, and that is just what happened to me that day. His words cut deep, and I was faced with what to do about the situation.

I could have tried to justify what I had done. After all, I *had* technically "paid" for all these clothes. I even had the receipts. But I knew that wouldn't wash, not in my mind or in my friends' minds, and certainly not in God's mind.

I realized at that moment that there were two very important issues at stake. First, I wanted to live a holy life before God because I knew that living the right kind of life is what keeps me in close fellowship with Him. Secondly, I wanted to be a consistent light to my friends, someone who would do what was right no matter what the personal cost. I wanted my friends to know that I wasn't just in some kind of "phase," that this wasn't just a religious experience that would fade as the year wore on. I wanted them to see that what I had was real and that it made a difference in my life.

It was time for me to draw my personal line of demarcation. I had to make a stand. My only course of action was to confess to my friend that I was wrong.

With my flesh crying out about how good I'd look in those nice, new clothes, I looked at my friends and said, "You're right. I was totally wrong to do what I've done tonight. But I don't want to put you guys on the spot, so here's what I'm going to do: you can have my share of this stuff, and you don't even have to pay me back for it. Do what you want with my share. I don't want any of these clothes."

I had no idea what my friends' response would be to that. For a moment, there was nothing but silence in that room. My friends just looked at me, and I could see in their eyes that they knew how serious I was about what I believed in. They realized at that moment that my relationship with God was more important to me than anything—including having nice clothes or having their approval.

I had made a stand in my own heart. I had laid down the law in my own life, and that law stated that from then on I would be completely submitted to God in everything I did and that nothing—not my family, not my friends, nobody—would come before God in my life. I knew at that point that every decision I made from then on would be made with submission to God's will in mind.

At that point, I felt as if God's anointing was on my life, simply because I had made a stand for Him. In hindsight, I can see that God's timing for these things couldn't possibly have been better, because my life was about to go through more major changes.

From then on, things were going to be much, much different.

PASS COVERAGE

1. Can you think of times when you knew God was arranging situations in order to bring you into His will? What were the circumstances?

2. Do you find it easy or difficult to submit yourself to someone who knows more about something than you do?

3. Who were the people who had the most influence on your decision to become a Christian? In what way did they influence you?

4. Have you ever had a nonbelieving friend or family member confront you with a sinful action or attitude? How did that make you feel? What did you do when you were confronted?

CHAPTER FIVE

MOVING ON AND UP

GETTING A SHOT AT THE NFL

"I am the LORD your God,
who teaches you what is best for you,
who directs you in the way you should go."

—ISAIAH 48:17

had a lot to look forward to as I spent the summer of 1990 preparing for my final year of football at Southern University.

My junior year had been a good one for me—better than I'd ever dreamed it could be when I first went out for football in the fall of 1988—and it raised within me the anticipation of a great senior season. In addition to that, I looked forward to a year in which I would move ever closer to what had now become a reachable goal for me: playing in the National Football League.

There was more to it than that, though.

I was also excited because my focus had changed. I was no longer playing just for myself or for my Southern University teammates or for a chance to play in the NFL. I was playing with the purpose of glorifying Jesus Christ.

With that newfound purpose in mind, I knew that the hand of God would be on me as I approached the season. I knew good things were going to happen.

Personal Praise

As a team, Southern struggled to a 4-7 record, losing several close games including my final matchup with Grambling State in the 1990 Bayou Classic. As much as it hurt to lose that game, it's still a great memory for me because I received an honor that is still a highlight in my football career. I was named the game's most valuable player. My dad still has the trophy at his home in New Orleans, and I doubt if he's going to let me take it home any time soon!

It's kind of a cliche, but it was true for me: I was in a zone. I was matched up with another future NFL player—wide receiver Jake Reed, currently with the Minnesota Vikings—and I shut him down. I made plays all over the field. I remember one play in particular, when I made a tackle by picking a guy up over my head and slamming him down to the Superdome turf. I'll never forget how the crowd erupted when I made that play.

I was blessed with an incredible senior season at Southern. My play got the attention of my teammates, coaches, and the local media, but it also got me attention I never thought I'd get when I started playing college football two years before. I'm talking about attention from the National Football League.

They're Talking about Me?

All season I heard talk about my status as a legitimate NFL prospect— from our coaches, opposing teams, in the newspapers and magazines, and from the league's scouts. Some of the things that were being said about me were, in a word, shocking.

It was strange to hear people describing me as "a potential first-round draft pick" and "one of the best defensive players in the nation," but at the same time it was confirmation to me of what I was starting to think was God's plan of a career in the NFL.

One of the most memorable of those confirmations came one day at one of our team meetings when Coach Percy Duhé, the Southern University defensive coordinator, told the team, "Men, we've got scouts hovering all over this place, and they tell me we've got the best defensive player in the country on our team. That player is Aeneas Williams."

Coach Duhé wasn't the kind of man to throw around compliments. In fact, he was one of the most demanding, hard-nosed, tell-it-like-it-is coaches I've ever played for. If you didn't know Coach Duhé, you might think he was one of the meanest men on earth. I didn't always enjoy the way he dealt with me, but I had—and still have—a lot of respect for the man. When I look back on how hard he was on us I can see that he was tough, but he was also fair. He never demanded anything of me or my teammates that he wasn't prepared to do himself.

I was in a state of shock to hear Coach Duhé say what he did that day. *I'm being talked about by NFL scouts that way?* I thought. It was nice to hear that I was an NFL prospect, but part of me still wondered if I was worthy of that kind of discussion.

Sure, I knew I was playing great football, but I also knew I was playing it at a relatively "small" Division 1-AA school and that NFL scouts preferred to see their prospects playing against the Division 1-A teams (you know, the "big boys").

It's in His Hands

Although I wondered where all this NFL talk would take me, I knew that God would ultimately decide whether or not I played professional football. With that in mind, I went about the business of playing for the Southern University Jaguars.

When I think back on that season, I can't help but see that God was in the middle of it all for me, orchestrating my future before my very eyes. It seemed like everything I touched turned to gold. I finished the season tied with Claude Pettaway, a safety from the University of Maine, for the Division 1-AA national lead in interceptions with eleven. In addition, I led the team in unassisted tackles and was credited with seventeen pass deflections.

I was also named a first-team All-Southwestern Athletic Conference selection, a Sheridan Black College All-America, and Sheridan Defensive Most Valuable Player. In addition, I was selected to play in the Senior Bowl all-star game.

I was happy with how God had blessed me with such a great season, and I was excited to think that He could further bless me with a chance to play in the NFL. I prayed a lot about what was ahead for me. Most of all, I prayed and asked God to remind me daily to remain submitted to His will for my life.

Having committed myself to that, it was time for me to get ready for the National Football League draft.

Where Will I Go?

Draft Day is one of those pivotal times in the life of any professional football player. It's a day he looks forward to with great anticipation—and sometimes with a feeling of dread, because he has no idea where he'll go, either in the order of the draft or to which team.

The 1991 draft had some quality players at my position—cornerback. Eric Turner of UCLA was projected to be a high first-round pick, as was Nebraska's Bruce Pickens. Notre Dame's Todd Lyght wasn't expected to have a long wait before his name was called either.

Where was I projected to go in the draft? It depended on who you talked to. I had been rated as one of the top collegiate defensive backs in the nation that year, and that had people thinking I would go in the first round. On the other hand, playing for a Division 1-AA school doesn't help a player who hopes to be a high draft pick. There's no question I was stigmatized a little by having played at a smaller school, but I also knew that a lot of quality NFL players come from smaller schools. For example, Mississippi Valley State, a school in the Southwestern Athletic Conference, produced a wide receiver by the name of Jerry Rice.

Most of the scouts I'd heard from said I could be drafted anywhere in the first three rounds with a legitimate chance of going in the first round.

As Draft Day 1991 approached, I felt nothing but peace and excitement over what everybody knew was coming for me, even if they—or I, for that matter—didn't know where. I can still remember people asking me about it, wanting to know if I was worried over where I would go or what I would do if the NFL didn't work out for me.

I wasn't. Not in the least.

I knew God was in control, and I was willing to go where He wanted me to go, when He wanted me to go there. I was completely at peace. He was in charge!

There was a small problem, though, a problem I more or less brought upon myself.

Stubbing My Toe

I hadn't exactly helped myself in the Senior Bowl or in the annual NFL Combine in Indianapolis. I played fairly well in the Senior Bowl game, but I didn't have very good practices. Practices, it turns out, is where the scouts watch the players. For some reason, I just wasn't comfortable at practice that week, and I knew there was a chance I'd hurt myself in the eyes of the scouts.

The NFL Combine is basically an annual meat market for aspiring pro football players. It's a chance for players to show their physical abilities through a series of drills. In the case of cornerbacks, the scouts at the Combine use speed, quickness, and jumping and breaking ability as the basis for evaluating a player's ability. What they don't use—and can't, in that setting—is coverage skills.

I didn't perform as well as I could have at the Combine. When NFL scouts look at cornerbacks, they're looking for guys with superhuman speed—in the 4.3–4.4 40 range. I had already run a 4.3 forty, but I didn't run that well that day—maybe a 4.5.

There's no other way to put it: I choked.

I knew what I was capable of doing, but that didn't stop that old enemy—fear—from keeping me from doing what I had already proved I could do. It's funny, looking back on it. I knew that God was in control of my career in professional football. But there was something about that new domain at the Combine that shook me up and made me nervous. I was outside my comfort zone, and I let the pressure get to me. For only a moment, I took my eyes off of who was in control and put them on my situation. Consequently, I let the pressure get the best of me.

Ironically, I found out later that going to the Combine probably wasn't in my best interests anyway, because the scouts already knew about me because of what I'd done in college the previous season. I'd had a great senior season, and the scouts were well aware of my abilities. I found out that a lot of players who were already considered high picks skip the Combine, knowing that they have more to lose than to gain if they happen to have a bad day.

The great thing about being submitted to the will of God, though, is that even when you make a mistake—even an unwitting one like mine—or have a bad day, He is still in control. God had a plan for me, and I believed that as long as I was submitted to Him, I'd land right where I belonged.

As Draft Day approached, I became less and less concerned about my bad showing at the Senior Bowl and the Combine. The way I saw it, I had always figured I'd be working for an accounting firm by this time in my life anyway. Having a shot at the National Football League was just frosting on the cake, an extra blessing.

I continued to work out to prepare my body for this next step. And I prayed that the peace of God—that peace where you just know He's in control and that you're in the center of His will—would continue in my heart and mind.

I'm happy to say that it did!

A Draft Day Party

Sunday, April 21, 1991, started out like any other Sunday for me since I'd submitted my life to Jesus Christ. I got up, went to church, then came home.

That's when things changed.

It seemed like everybody I knew was at Mom and Dad's house in New Orleans, ready to support me and encourage me while I waited to be picked and to congratulate me and celebrate with me once I was chosen. I still have a special fondness and appreciation for my family and friends being there for me. It was a great time for everybody.

Everybody wanted to know how I was feeling, where I thought I'd be drafted, and if I was nervous. The answers to those questions were, in order:

at peace, wherever God wanted me to be, and not at all.

Considering how big of a day that was for me, it might sound hard to believe, but I wasn't in the least worried or nervous about anything. For me, it was a win-win situation. I'd already seen the power of God in my life—on the football field and off—and I knew He'd put me in the right place at the right time. I was excited to know where that place was, and before that Sunday afternoon was over, I'd know.

A Lot of Hoopla

The NFL Draft has become quite an event in the world of sports, thanks in no small part to ESPN, the cable sports station. They put on an elaborate show, with Chris Berman providing the play by play—if you want to call it that—and a whole host of analysts and commentators giving their take on each and every pick. In addition, ESPN has reporters at every team's draft "war room," ready to get the latest commentary from the league's coaches and management.

My friends, family, and I all gathered around the TV to watch the show, and when the Dallas Cowboys announced that they were selecting defensive tackle Russell Maryland of the University of Miami with the first pick in the 1991 Draft, the wait was officially on for us.

I was excited to see where I would go, and curious to see where everybody else would go too. It was like Christmas morning! I knew that several teams—including the Buffalo Bills, Denver Broncos, and Kansas City Chiefs—had expressed interest in me, but I really had no clue where I'd be going.

The first round proceeded with cornerbacks Eric Turner going to Cleveland with the second overall selection, Bruce Pickens of Nebraska going with the third pick to Atlanta, linebacker Mike Croel of Nebraska going to Denver at number four, and Todd Lyght going fifth to the Los Angeles Rams. That was three cornerbacks in the first five picks!

When the first round of the draft ended, my name still hadn't been called. When the second round drew to a close, I could feel the nervousness in the room. Nobody was saying much, but I'm sure some people there were starting to get a little worried. I'm not going to tell you I wasn't feeling a little excited. I was still at peace, but ever more curious about what would happen. I had a feeling my time was coming.

It was near, too. Shortly after the second round came to a close—and ESPN's coverage ended—I got a phone call informing me I'd been taken with the fourth pick of the third round—the fifty-ninth pick overall. The team? The Phoenix Cardinals.

The Cardinals official I talked to on the phone told me that they had taken me with their third pick in that year's draft. He congratulated me and told me they were looking forward to working with me and that they were looking for big things out of me.

After I hung up the phone, I made the announcement to my friends and family: I was going to be a Phoenix Cardinal.

A Chance to Play—Immediately

Other than the fact that they had recently moved to Phoenix from St. Louis (that move was actually in the spring of 1988 and came after the team had spent twenty-eight years in St. Louis), I didn't know a whole lot about the Cardinals when I was drafted.

They hadn't been one of the premier teams in the league since their move to Phoenix, but they'd had some good years in St. Louis. With players like quarterback Jim Hart, halfback Terry Metcalf, and wide receiver Mel Gray spearheading their offense, the then St. Louis Cardinals had put together a string of three good years (playoff appearances in 1974 and 1975) in the mid-1970s. Since that time, they had struggled, finishing with winning records only three times.

Although I wasn't going to a team with an established winning record, my enthusiasm for what was about to happen in my life wasn't dampened a bit. It was an exciting time for me. I looked forward to the challenge, not just of playing in the National Football League, but of helping to turn a losing team around.

Cardinals Coach Joe Bugel was entering his second season with the team, and he appeared ready to make some changes in player personnel after the Cardinals had posted two 5-11 seasons. One of those changes was in the defensive backfield, where, with the exception of All-Pro strong safety Tim McDonald, all the positions were up for grabs. It looked like I would have a great chance of stepping in and playing—maybe even as a starter—my first year with the Cardinals.

It amazes me to think about how God orchestrated my being picked by the Cardinals. They turned out to be the perfect team for me to go to. Not only would I have a chance to make the team and play, but I'd be bucking for a starting spot right away.

Now, it was up to me. The next step was beating out the competition on the team to get that starting spot.

Earning a Spot

If for no other reason than the numbers—we were going to have twelve defensive backs coming in when training camp opened—I knew it was going to be a competitive training camp for the Cardinals. Cedric Mack and Jay Taylor were the returning starting cornerbacks, with Lorenzo Lynch also pushing for playing time. The team also had Marcus Turner at cornerback and was trying to get Lonnie Young, the starting free safety, to practice at corner. In addition to that, the Cardinals had drafted four defensive backs, including me, Dexter Davis of Clemson in the fourth round, and Herbie Anderson of Texas A & M in the tenth. All three of us played the cornerback spot.

Getting My Feet Wet

My first experience in the NFL was the Phoenix Cardinals' minicamp, which was held during the first week of May. That's where the rookies and most of the veterans get together for a three-day camp in order to get everyone acquainted with one another.

I was a little nervous when the minicamp started, but that didn't last long. Remember, I had trained with some professional players, including Maurice Hurst, during the summer between my junior and senior seasons in college, so I wasn't too overwhelmed to see the level of play at the minicamp.

I played pretty well at minicamp. I covered people well and made some good plays. After I returned home, I continued to train in preparation for the upcoming free agent and rookie camp that June in Phoenix.

I had a great rookie camp, too, making play after play and impressing the Cardinals defensive backs' coach, Jim Johnson. As the rookie camp ended, I couldn't wait for the 1991 Phoenix Cardinals training camp to start. The only problem was, I'd be getting a late start while my agent negotiated with the Cardinals to work out my contract.

Enduring a Holdout

Nobody—not the management, not the coaches, and certainly not the players—enjoys a contractual holdout. It's a time when management can be seen as the tightwad heavy and the players can be seen as spoiled money-grubbers. Unfortunately, holdouts are a fact of life in the NFL.

I had to hold out for about two weeks during the Cardinals' 1991 training camp while my agent worked out a contract. I didn't enjoy the holdout, but I was patient and at peace with what we were doing. I understood that this is the business aspect of professional football, and I was grateful that I had an agent to take care of it for me.

I continued to work out while I waited. Fortunately, I had four NFL cornerbacks—Kevin Lewis, Maurice Hurst, Randy Hilliard of Cleveland, and Gary Lewis of the Los Angeles Raiders—available to work out with me. We spent hours and hours going over drills and working on footwork at Tulane University in New Orleans.

Finally, my agent and the Cardinals came to an agreement. I was officially a member of the Phoenix Cardinals. It was time to move on to my first National Football League training camp.

Will I Make It?

When I set my goals as far as my football career is concerned, I like to set them one at a time. When I accomplish the first one, I move on. Once my contract holdout was over, my first goal was simply making the Arizona Cardinals football team.

As I headed to Arizona for training camp, I was still confident in my ability to play in the NFL. What I wondered about, though, was if my holdout would hurt not only my chances of starting that year but my chances of making the team. Some of the Phoenix coaches, while they liked my ability, wondered the same thing.

It wasn't long before I felt right at home in the Cardinals' defensive backfield. Within a week, I was out making plays like I'd never missed a day of camp. I was covering our best receivers and making play after play at practice. Before I knew it, I had been promoted to the third cornerback spot on the Cardinals' depth chart.

I played well throughout that first training camp, and I felt complete confidence in what I was doing. But as we got down to the last week, I still wondered what the coaches' plans were for me.

Instead of waiting, I came right out and asked.

I walked up to Coach Johnson one day near the end of training camp and asked him, "I'm thinking about buying an apartment in town and I need to know before I purchase it what my chances are of making the team."

Coach Johnson looked at me and he said, "Not only are you going to make the team, but you're starting at cornerback."

The following day, the Cardinals released Cedric Mack, who had been a starter at cornerback for the previous six seasons. I felt bad to see Cedric released (he signed with another team and played a few more years in the league), but I was elated to be promoted to the starting lineup.

It amazed me to think how one day before I asked Coach Johnson about my status with the team I wasn't totally sure if I'd even make the team, and now I was a starter. At that point I realized I had accomplished my first goal—that of making the team. Now it was time to set newer, higher goals.

Bigger and Better Things

When I started my NFL career as a rookie with the Phoenix Cardinals in 1991, I wasn't thinking about biding my time on the bench and learning. I wanted to step in and start right away. With that goal achieved, I set for myself some higher goals: I wanted to lead the league in interceptions and to be named the league's rookie of the year.

Those were some lofty goals, to be sure, but I believed in my heart that they were attainable for me.

Setting those kinds of goals is something I do in order to challenge myself, to get myself to try to do things I might not otherwise think I was capable of doing. I always say that I try to shoot for the moon, and if I miss, I hit a few stars.

I hit more than my share during my rookie season.

A Splashy Debut

We were scheduled to open the season against a team that would give our defensive backfield quite a test: the Los Angeles Rams. The Rams featured one of the best crews of receivers in the NFL. Henry Ellard, the future Hall of Famer, and Willie "Flipper" Anderson were both coming off 1,000-yard seasons for the Rams, and Aaron Cox was a dangerous third receiver. Quarterback Jim Everett had been playing incredible football the previous three seasons, throwing for more than 12,000 yards and eighty-three touchdowns during that time. Obviously, our defensive backs had their work cut out for them.

I was nervous when I headed out on the field at Anaheim Stadium, but at the same time I had inside me a sense of peace. I knew that if I laid aside my own nervousness and fear and moved ahead with what I knew I could do, that God was going to bless me.

I knew beyond any doubt that God had brought me to the point He had for a purpose. I knew that He wanted to use me as a player in the National Football League.

That's something I've learned that applies in every area of my life: if I go forward in spite my own fears and anxiety, God will do extraordinary things in and through me. God doesn't always take away my nervousness or fear, but He gives me enough courage to go out and "do it scared." It's like a personal promise God has made to me, and He's always kept it. My first NFL game was no exception.

I prayed for the peace of God to be on me as I prepared for my first regular season game. Then it was time to play.

Being the rookie cornerback on our team, the Rams threw at me a lot. They were doing what any NFL team does: they were picking on the rookie. It doesn't matter what kind of reputation you have coming out of college, if you're a rookie cornerback, they're going to throw the ball in your direction.

I didn't stop every pass that came my way, but I had a great first outing, including my first interception. I got the pick when safety Tim McDonald tipped one of Jim Everett's passes and it came floating my direction. I'll never forget the feeling I had when I got that first interception. When I got up off the turf and headed off the field, I held onto the ball like my life depended on it. No one was going to get it away from me.

My interception helped the Cardinals to a 24-14 win over the Rams. The following week against Philadelphia at Veterans Stadium, I had an interception and a fumble recovery—both plays stopped Eagle scoring threats—to help us win 26-10 and go 2-0.

After the 2-0 start, we won only two more games that season, finishing 4-12 after losing our final eight games.

We had some close losses, including one memorable game against the Denver Broncos at Mile High Stadium in which I had two interceptions off John Elway for my first two-interception game. Both picks set up scores for the Cardinals, but we still lost 24-19. Despite the loss, it was a thrilling accomplishment to get two interceptions off a quarterback of the stature of John Elway. I had—and still have—a lot of respect for him, and I felt blessed to have such a great day against him.

I had a busy rookie year at my cornerback spot. It seemed that there wasn't a team we played that didn't try to break me down. I enjoyed the challenge of being thrown at all year, and I more than held my own. I started 15 games (I missed the start in our third game because of a twisted ankle, but I still played most of the game), finishing with a share of the National Football Conference lead in interceptions with six. There were very few times that season when I was beaten, and we tied as a team for the league lead with Buffalo, New Orleans, and Denver for fewest touchdown passes given up.

Earning Respect

I fell short of achieving my goal of leading the NFL in interceptions—that honor went to safety Ronnie Lott of the Raiders with eight picks—and I wasn't named the league's rookie of the year, but I was named the NFC Defensive Rookie of the Year by the NFL Players Association.

It was a huge honor for me to be recognized by my peers as the top rookie defender in the NFC, and it showed me what can happen when I apply myself and allow my willingness to sacrifice myself to speak for itself. By just working hard and doing the things I needed to do to succeed—including submitting to the direction of my coaches—I had earned the respect of my peers as a football player, and that meant a lot to me.

What meant even more, though, is that my peers understood what made me the player I was in 1991 and that they understood that my success on the football field wasn't going to change what God had made me to be when He saved me two years before.

Tim McDonald, who has since moved on to play for the San Francisco 49ers, once approached me in the locker room and said, "You know, Aeneas, it seems like you're ahead of your time in how you approach things."

I believed then—and I believe now—that Tim saw in the way I carried myself the same things that God had placed in my heart during those first few years I lived as a saved man, those same things that have helped me to be a success in the NFL. Tim saw in me what I call the "spirit of excellence," which means that no matter what I'm doing I'm doing it as for God. It means that I'm following the scriptural mandate that says, "And whatever you do, whether in word or deed, do it all in the name of the Lord Jesus, giving thanks to God the Father through him" (Colossians 3:17).

It was that spirit of excellence that motivated me to work as hard as I did, to go the extra mile in practice, to study game films late after practice, and to keep my focus on playing the best football I was capable of playing. It motivated me to want to be the best cornerback I could possibly be so that I could glorify the Lord in the work I did.

I believe that Tim and the rest of my teammates also recognized that while I was a confident player, I wasn't arrogant. They may not have fully understood what gave me that confidence, but they could see in me that I knew what I could do and never backed down from a challenge.

It was because I was submitted to God that I was secure and confident in what I was doing on the football field. And I would need every bit of that security and confidence as I embarked on what would be a challenging, trying second year in the National Football League.

But before I moved on to my second season, God was going to get started on making a huge change in my life, a change that would teach me even more about the importance of submitting myself to godly authority.

PASS COVERAGE

1. Do you approach everything you do with an attitude of service for Christ? If so, what difference has that made in your performance. If not, why not?

2. How do you respond when someone says something complimentary to you?

3. If you had your choice, would you rather go to a situation where things would be easy or to one where you would be challenged? Why?

4. How do you respond when you receive recognition for something you've done well?

◄ TAKING A HUGE STEP ►

THE ULTIMATE IN EARTHLY SUBMISSION: MARRIAGE

A wife of noble character who can find?
She is worth far more than rubies.
Her husband has full confidence in her
and lacks nothing of value.

—PROVERBS 31:10–11

'****'ve got some advice for you if you're thinking about getting married.
Don't do it!
Don't do it, that is, unless it's to the right person. Don't do it unless you know that God has shown you that the one you want to marry is the right woman for you. Don't do it if you yourself aren't ready for big changes in your life. Don't do it if you and your potential mate don't both understand the importance of respect for authority.

The Bible says in Proverbs 18:22, "He who finds a wife finds what is good and receives favor from the LORD." I'm a living example of that. I have definitely found something good in my wife, Tracy. She is, in every way, a reminder to me that I have found favor from God.

I can tell you, marriage is a good thing. Marriage is a good thing because it's God's idea, not man's. It was His idea from the beginning.

Marriage: God's Idea

From the moment God first created Adam, He never intended for the man to be alone. At first, though, Adam didn't know what God's plans were. Back in the Garden of Eden, Adam looked around and noticed something:

All the animals had mates, yet he was alone. For every ram there was a ewe. For every buck there was a doe. For every bull there was a cow. Yet Adam had nobody.

God was way ahead of Adam. He even said, "It is not good for the man to be alone," then He did something about it. At just the right time, God brought Adam a mate. The Bible says that God caused Adam to go to sleep, then took from him a rib out of which he fashioned the woman.

The woman was the perfect mate for Adam in every way. She was remarkably like Adam, yet remarkably different from him. She could think, talk, and walk like him, but in ways that were somehow different. She was a perfect complement to Adam and the completion of a wonderful plan of God's—the plan of marriage.

Whenever I read the account of the creation of man and woman in the Book of Genesis, I'm all the more grateful for my marriage relationship with my wife, Tracy. I'm grateful that God has brought to me my perfect complement.

That doesn't mean that being married has always been easy for us. Nothing that is worth doing is easy, and marriage is no exception. It's the union of two imperfect people who need the grace of God to be able to share their lives with another person.

Two Imperfect Partners

I love my wife more than anything in the world, but getting married was a huge adjustment for me. It's a huge adjustment for anybody—even for someone who has a strong relationship with the Lord—and it can become a disastrous situation if the person you choose to marry is wrong for you. And it can be even worse if you haven't prepared yourself for the changes that lie ahead when you take a wife.

It's amazing the things you learn about yourself when you get married. During those first few years of living under the same roof with that person you promised to love forever is when the blind spots in your character start to be exposed. For example, when you're single you may think of yourself as the most giving person in the world, but when you get married you find out about your selfishness.

When you're single, the only person you have to worry about is you. You come home and there's no one there to bother you or change your plans for that night. When you get married, though, someone comes in and totally changes all that. Now, you share everything you have and everything you are with this other person.

It can be a shock to the system to learn those things about yourself, and going through that can be downright miserable if you're not married to the right person. Believe me, I know a lot of guys who are in that position. Sadly, a lot of their marriages don't make it.

I feel extremely blessed that I'm not one of those guys. I am blessed to be married to the woman who I know, beyond any doubt, is the one God wanted me to marry.

Looking in the Right Place

I first met Tracy through Marcus Williams, a friend of mine at Southern University who was dating her twin sister, Stacy. Our first meeting was very brief—in fact, I don't think we said much of anything to each other. I knew I wanted to see her again, though, and I found myself looking for her around the campus and around the places I'd heard she hung out. Somehow I knew I would find her and eventually I did.

I finally made contact with Tracy at the annual convocation, at Southern University where the president speaks to the entire student body. I went, somehow knowing I would see her there. I did. It was the moment I'd been waiting for, and I didn't waste it, either. I walked over to her and started a conversation. I didn't ask her out or even ask for her phone number, but I found out where I could contact her again.

I talked to her again several times, eventually getting up the nerve to ask her out on a date. It didn't take long for me to see how different she was. It also didn't take me long to realize that my feelings for her were different too.

A Special Lady

Almost from the moment I first met Tracy, I just knew she was the lady for me. She was special to me from the moment I met her, not just because I liked her personality and thought she was beautiful, but because of the deep respect I had for her. I respected what Tracy stood for, and I respected how her life was different from most people I knew at Southern University.

I respected how Tracy put her relationship with God and the values that relationship instilled in her ahead of everything—including me. Her parents had also taught her she was precious, and that any man who wanted her was going to have to wait for sexual intimacy until they got married. She wasn't about to give up what she knew to be right for some football player, and she wasn't about to give herself emotionally to a man whose beliefs weren't the same as hers.

The problem at first is that I wasn't living the same kind of life she was. I didn't know her God, and I certainly didn't understand what kind of life this God wanted me to lead. But through Tracy's witness—and the witness of my friend and former high school football teammate, Kevin Lewis—I came to a point in my life where I knew that God wanted a relationship with me and that I could have that relationship because of what Jesus Christ had done for me 2,000 years ago on the cross.

My having made a commitment to Christ changed me in more ways than I can count, but it also changed my relationship with Tracy. While before there was something amiss between us—she knew Jesus and I didn't—there was now a closeness, a bond that can only occur between two people who are filled with and controlled by the Spirit of God. We now had in common the most important thing in the world: a relationship with the Lord.

My relationship with Tracy continued to grow during my final year at Southern University and during my first year with the Phoenix Cardinals. We were apart for much of that year, but my love for her continued to grow. It was at the end of that year that I realized something: I wanted to make Tracy a permanent part of my life. I wanted to marry her.

I was growing in my spiritual life at that time, but I was struggling with that old enemy—fear. I had an intense inner struggle as I contemplated what it meant to get married. I wanted to marry Tracy, but there was a part of me that didn't want to take that next step and commit myself to her.

Eventually, with the help of a dear old friend (I'll talk about him at length later on), I overcame that fear and asked Tracy Smith if she would be my wife.

Will You Marry Me?

Tracy and I had already talked a lot about getting married when I took her one beautiful New Orleans evening to a restaurant called Augie's Glass Garden. We'd talked about what it would be like to live together in a marriage, what kind of adjustments we'd have to make. We even talked about how many children we'd have and what we'd name them. (Our first daughter's name is Saenea, which is "Aeneas" spelled backwards. We're keeping our first son's name a secret until we have him, so don't ask.)

I think Tracy sensed something big was going to happen. There was probably something in the way I was acting that let her know that I was a little nervous because this wasn't going to be just any night out on the town.

I had asked the waitress to put the ring on the dessert tray, and she brought it out after we had finished dinner. When she showed us the tray, there was the ring. The rest was up to me. I took the ring, got down on one knee next to Tracy's chair, and asked her if she would marry me.

The answer was an enthusiastic "yes!"

We later set the wedding date for after my second season with the Cardinals. Then we prepared to be apart again. I headed back to Phoenix and Tracy headed to the University of Illinois.

It was tough being away from Tracy so much that year. She wrote letters, I called (I'm not much of a letter writer), and we got together as much as we could. Whether we were together or apart, we both looked forward to our wedding day.

Finally, the big day came. We were married on January 9, 1992, a few months after the end of my second season with the Cardinals. The ceremony was at Tracy's home church, the Hartzell Mt. Zion United Methodist Church in her hometown of Slidell, Louisiana, followed by a reception in New Orleans.

Our wedding was pretty typical in every way but one: it was *our* wedding, and we knew from then on things were going to be a lot different in both our lives.

Yes, my decision to marry Tracy was the second biggest one I'd ever made—behind giving my life to Jesus Christ—and a decision I've never regretted.

And it's a decision that I'd recommend—as long as you've found the right woman, the one of God's choosing, to marry.

And how, you might ask, do you know if you've found the right one? Well, I'm no expert, but I've learned by being married to Tracy the qualities in a woman that you can't go wrong looking for.

Finding "the One"

If there's one thing I'd tell any Christian man who is thinking about getting married, it would be this: make sure this young woman is living a submitted, committed life for Jesus Christ. If she's not, then the Bible says explicitly that this person is not for you: "Do not be yoked together with unbelievers. For what do righteousness and wickedness have in common? Or what fellowship can light have with darkness?" (2 Corinthians 6:14).

It is not only important that your potential wife be committed to Jesus Christ; it's absolutely crucial. On a purely practical level, it's crucial because marriage is tough enough without being married to someone who doesn't share what should be the most important part of your life.

There's more to it than that, though. If you're married to an unbeliever, it keeps you from accomplishing many of the things you should be accomplishing for God. Being married to someone who isn't a believer keeps you from the ministry God sets before you—and if you know Jesus, He *will* give you a ministry—simply because you're now in a position of using all your spiritual energy just trying to get your wife saved.

If you think that will work, consider the fact that the apostle Paul repeatedly likens the Christian life to running a marathon, then think about what it would be like to run that marathon with an anchor tied around your neck. Obviously, that would put you at a disadvantage!

On the other hand, when you are married to a committed, submitted believer, you don't have to worry about making sure your wife will one day be in heaven. Instead, you will find that you and your wife actually challenge one another to grow spiritually. The great thing about being married to a woman of God like Tracy is that she challenges me to grow in my relationship with the Lord. The more I see her grow—and I see that almost daily—the more I want to grow. And the more I grow, the more she feels challenged to grow. It's the wonderful part of two people being married who are committed to the Lord, and I know it will continue with us as we grow old together.

Seeking Maturity

Since both Tracy and I had committed our lives to Christ before we got married, we had a measure of spiritual maturity. We had by no means "arrived" in our walks with the Lord—I don't believe that will happen in this lifetime—but we had a foundation of maturity.

Spiritual maturity is important in a marriage, especially in times of conflict. It may be hard for you to believe when you're looking at that beautiful young woman and thinking how you can't wait to be married that there will come a time in your marital relationship when you have conflicts. Tracy and I had conflicts at different times in our marriage, but the good news is that we've been able—with the help of the Lord—to work through those challenges. We've been able to do that simply because we both have that foundation of submission to Jesus Christ.

What helps Tracy and me get through our conflicts and challenges is that we both understand that marriage is a covenant—an agreement between God and us that we will love one another and stand by one another no matter what happens and no matter what differences may arise between us. In short, divorce is not an option.

Marriage is a divine institution in which two people make a commitment—each to someone who is an imperfect human being who thinks differently and reacts differently to different situations, and you need that foundation of maturity to be able to respond well to one another's differences.

I've realized through being married that if we could understand and accept the fact that God made men and women differently it would help us to handle our marital conflicts better. It would help men and women both to appreciate the fact that God made each gender different for a reason, and it would help them to appreciate those differences rather than try to change them.

It took a lot of pressure off our relationship once I realized that my wife—because of our differences in upbringing and background, and simply because I'm a man and she's a woman—thinks and responds differently to different situations and different topics than I do. It helped me to understand that those differences didn't necessarily make me right and her wrong, or vice versa, but only pointed out a different perspective between the two of us. Once I understood this, I realized that when my wife and I disagree about something, it isn't necessarily because we're both trying to get our own way and it doesn't necessarily mean we're at odds with one another about what ultimately needs to be done.

A good example of this occurred recently when we needed some repairs done on the roof of our house. I called about three different roofers for estimates and made an appointment for one of them to come to our home.

Before I went to work that day, I gave Tracy specific instructions. I told her the name of the roofer and what time he was coming over, then left.

When I got home, I asked her, "How did it go? Did the roofer show up?"

"Oh, it went really well. The roofer came here and did the work, and I paid him."

It was true. The roofer came, did the work we needed done, got paid, and left. The only problem was that it was the wrong roofer. For some reason, one of the other roofers I had talked to showed up earlier than he said he would, and Tracy let him do the work and paid him.

Being a man—an instruction- and goal-oriented male human being—I started to feel angry at my wife because I thought she had ignored my instructions. But the Holy Spirit almost immediately spoke to my heart and pointed out to me that my wife hadn't ignored my instructions, and she hadn't tried to pull anything on me. It was simply a case of miscommunication.

The bottom line was that we both had the same goal in mind: to repair the roof. While the way I had planned for that to take place hadn't occurred, the job still got done (although I'm sure the other roofer was probably wondering what I had been thinking).

That incident taught me a lot about how Tracy and I can have the same goal but disagree—even if it wasn't intentional—on how to get it done. It also taught me a lot about our submission to one another when we're trying to accomplish something.

Submitting One to Another

I don't think you could write a book—or even a chapter within a book—about the subject of marriage without bringing in that oft-quoted verse, "Wives, submit to your husbands as to the Lord" (Ephesians 5:22).

It sounds badly outdated in some circles to talk about wives submitting to husbands in 1990s America. It seems that nobody wants to submit to anything or anybody these days, especially women to their husbands.

A lot of the reason for that, I believe, is that the word *submission* has been so often misused. In our culture, being submitted has come to mean that you've put yourself in a master/slave relationship with someone who wants to run your life and put you in a position of servitude. That is the basis of some people's criticism of the Promise Keepers, the ministry that encourages men to be better husbands and fathers. Well, that criticism is dead wrong. It is, in fact, a deception from the devil.

The Word is pretty clear about it: Wives are to submit to the authority of their husbands. A lot of women don't like to hear that, but it's truth. It's the Word of God. And it works—if both parties are committed to filling their marital roles as God has laid them out in the Bible.

Sadly, many women—those who don't understand this concept or those who are married to men who don't understand it—wouldn't submit to anybody, especially their husbands. Instead, they choose to get in the forefront and do what their husbands are called to do: lead.

I think we Christian men deserve a lot of the blame for that. There aren't too many of us who are worth submitting to, because we demand respect and submission without doing what it takes to deserve it. We look at Ephesians 5:22 and think that our wives and children will blindly submit to us when we haven't submitted our own lives to the authority of God.

The biggest mistake men make is taking the attitude that he's going to demand respect from his wife and demand that she submit to him. That just won't work. You can't demand respect, and if you do you're asking for trouble. Respect and submission are earned through the content of your character, and that content of character comes only when you yourself are submitted to God.

If you want a happy marriage, your wife has to see in you a committed, submitted relationship with God. She has to see you being willing to do the things that bring you closer to God and to her. She has to see you with a heart that wants to serve God and your family. Any woman who sees that kind of submission in her husband will be more prone to submit to him, simply because that man is a figure who makes her feel loved and secure. Without that, he's nothing more than a stern authority figure.

But there's more, men. Not only do you need to submit your lives to God, you need to submit yourself to your wife. You might ask, "Where does it say in the Bible that a man is to submit to his wife?" While the Bible doesn't explicitly say, "Husbands, submit to your wives," it does say in Ephesians 5:21—one verse before the verse that says "Wives, submit to your husbands"—"Submit to one another out of reverence for Christ." That's a verse that applies to all of us—including us husbands.

But there's another Scripture that I've applied to this area of my life. It's in Galatians 6:7, where Paul writes: "A man reaps what he sows." I know that if I sow submission at home, submission is what I'm going to reap. On the other hand, if I sow pride, anger, selfishness, and stubbornness, that's exactly what I'm going to reap.

Mutual Submission

I believe that part of the reason Tracy and I are happily married is that I'm as submitted to her as she is to me. I have submitted myself to be completely accountable for the decisions I make and for my attitudes and actions as a husband and father.

Part of our submission to one another is that there isn't a decision made in our household that we don't discuss with one another. My wife and I both have total confidence that we will communicate with one another, that there are no unilateral decisions. And when I talk about communication, I don't mean that I communicate with her what the decision will be; I mean that she and I will do whatever it takes to come to an agreement on how we accomplish our goals. We make sure that we are, as the Bible puts it, "of one mind."

When I'm faced with a decision—concerning the family, my career, or in whatever area I have to decide something—I ask Tracy for her opinion about what I should do. I've always respected my wife as an intelligent, insightful woman, but I'm still amazed at times at the answers she gives when I ask her about something. In fact, I'm not in the least bit ashamed to say that a lot of the ideas I've gotten credit for over the years were Tracy's!

My wife is a very strong person—strong in character, strong in personality, strong in intellect, and strong in spirit. While many men are threatened by this kind of strength in a woman, I see it as a benefit to me, to her, and to our family. Instead of trying to overcome her strength, I want to utilize it to further the potential that we have as a family and as individuals. When that happens, there's no telling how much we can accomplish for the Lord!

Asking for a Critique

Part of utilizing Tracy's strength is that I often ask her how I'm doing as a husband, a father, and a spiritual leader. I ask her where I'm falling short and what I can do to improve. I honestly want to know, because I want to make my family the best it can be. Tracy recognizes this, and she responds to that desire by being honest with me. She tells me what I'm doing well, but she also lets me know where I fall short. And when she speaks, I listen!

When I fall short in some area as a husband and father, I immediately repent. I don't wait around. I turn to God right away and ask His forgiveness. I ask God to cleanse me of whatever attitude caused me to fall short in a given area. Then I go to my wife and, if need be, my daughter and confess that I've fallen short. The next step is to take the steps necessary to correct the situation.

Being married to a godly, loving, strong woman like Tracy has been a blessing to me far beyond anything I could have expected before I got married. She's my source of inspiration, comfort, and encouragement. I love her, respect her, and appreciate her in every way.

She helps me to be the man God calls me to be!

We're Responsible!

Whether or not our culture likes it, we men are responsible for the state of our homes. That's the way God made it, and that's the way it is. And if we can bring the way we relate to our wives and children in submission to the Lord and accept the responsibilities that God has given us as heads of our households, then we'll reap the kind of results we want.

My job as a husband and father is to humble myself and to be the servant of my wife and daughter. Ephesians 5:25 says, "Husbands, love your wives, just as Christ loved the church and gave himself up for her." And how did Christ love the church? By serving. He humbled Himself and served us to the point where He gave Himself up as a sacrifice for sins. That's the kind of self-sacrificing love that the Word says we are to have for our wives and children.

That's the kind of husband I want to be, and it's also the kind of father I want to be to my daughter, Saenea. It helps that I have Tracy as a wife, because she's not just a great wife, she's an incredible mother. And she challenges me to be a good father.

Being Mom and Dad

I'd been living with my beautiful wife for just five years when God blessed me by bringing into my life another beautiful little lady. On March 26, 1997, Tracy and I became the proud parents of our first child, Saenea.

Getting married changed our lives in so many ways that it's hard to list them. But becoming parents brought about just that many more changes for us. When Saenea came into the picture, it was like Tracy and I started a whole new life—again.

Children are a blessing from God, but they are also a huge responsibility. When you become parents, you are responsible for your child's every need: physical, emotional, intellectual, and spiritual. During those first few years of life, there's almost nothing that child will need that he or she will receive apart from the parents.

Those are some huge responsibilities, and none of them is any bigger than the responsibility of providing spiritual training for the child. And it's a responsibility that must be carried out twenty-four hours a day, seven days a week.

The Word of God tells us in Proverbs 22:6, "Train a child in the way he should go, and when he is old he will not turn from it." That tells us that kids will be what they're taught to be when they become adults. To me, though, there's more to it than that. To me, "when they're old" applies to the very day after I teach my daughter something. In other words, it means that what I teach my daughter in my words and actions will take effect immediately.

Spiritual training is like that because it happens not just when you say it to your kids, but when you do it in front of them. Kids know hypocrisy when they see it. I'm convinced they can tell when Mommy and Daddy aren't behaving the same way they want the kids to behave. When that happens, you've got trouble.

In a way, children are a microcosm of their parents, because they will always exhibit the kind of character and behavior they see at home. If Mom and Dad scream and yell at each other to try to get their own way, that's what the children learn to do. If Mom and Dad curse and lie and cheat, the kids will curse and lie and cheat. If Mom and Dad drink and smoke, their sons and daughters will drink and smoke.

On the other hand, if Mom and Dad live their lives committed to God and to loving and respecting one another and submitting to one another, then there's a pretty good chance the kids will grow up doing the same thing.

It's vital that you consistently live what you say, but it's all the more important when you become a parent. Your actions are going to speak louder than your words, so it's only a matter of what your actions say to the kids.

The key word in all of this is "consistent." Kids need to see Mom and Dad living out what they believe both in public and at home where nobody on the outside can see. Unfortunately, too many men are more concerned about how they look in public than how they look to their wife and kids. If the two are contradictory, it's just a matter of time before the family blows up. Dad can use the iron fist to control the situation for awhile, but eventually he'll lose control. When that happens, it's a lot like what happens when you hold a rubber ball under water and then let it go. When you let go of the ball, it rushes to the surface where it wants to be in the first place. After that, it drifts wherever the wind takes it.

Tracy and I are committed to making certain that our daughter—and, in the future, the rest of our children—sees us walking our walk before God no matter what we're doing and no matter where we are. We never want our daughter to be able to look at us and think, *Your actions are speaking so loud that I can't hear what you're saying.*

Take It Seriously!

Yes, being a husband and a father is a huge responsibility, one you should take very, very seriously before you decide to marry and start a family.

I can tell you from experience that it helps when you marry a woman who loves God and is committed to living for Him. But I can also tell you that it helps tremendously if you've submitted to God yourself.

In fact, it's the only way to go.

PASS COVERAGE

1. What are some of the things that scare you when you think about getting married?

2. What are some of your criteria for a potential wife?

3. What are some of the potential problems with getting married to an unbeliever?

4. How important is it for a wife to submit to her husband? How important is it for a husband to submit to his wife?

CHAPTER SEVEN

THE UPS AND DOWNS OF THE NFL

RESPONDING TO ADVERSITY

Although the Lord gives you the bread of adversity and the water of affliction,
your teachers will be hidden no more; with your own eyes you will see them.

—ISAIAH 30:20

I was blessed with a tremendous rookie season, a year in which I accomplished more than my status as a third-round draft pick might suggest. The challenge to me as I headed into my second season was to "prove it," to show people around the NFL that I wasn't a "one-year-wonder" or that my performance was some kind of fluke.

There's no question in my mind that I caught some people around the NFL by surprise during my rookie season. That wasn't going to happen my second year. It was a year in which teams were on to what I could do, and they had started game-planning for me—designing their offenses to either exploit me or avoid me.

I had been warned about that, and I knew I was going to have my work cut out for me if I was going to come even close to what I'd accomplished in my first year.

I had a strong preseason, and it looked like I'd avoid what is commonly called the "sophomore slump," an affliction that seems to be common to a lot of second-year players who've had big rookie seasons. The early part of my second season, however, included a stretch of games that was one of the most difficult times I'd ever endured as a football player.

It started in our second game of the year, a nationally televised game against Philadelphia at Sun Devil Stadium.

The Toast of Arizona

The game against the Eagles was one of the toughest of my life. It was embarrassing and frustrating. In the long run, though, it was good for me. It was, in fact, a game that changed the course of my career.

I was matched up against wide receiver Fred Barnett, who was in his third year in the league and who had been establishing a reputation as an explosive, big-play receiver. It was supposed to be one of the key matchups in the game, but it was no contest. Fred lit me up like a Christmas tree, finishing with eight catches for 193 yards and two touchdowns—both of which came right in front of me—in a 31-14 Eagles' win. He beat me mercilessly, play after play, and it seemed like there was nothing I could do about it. It was like I wasn't even on the field. It was the most embarrassing time I've ever had on a football field.

The week that followed that game was a challenging one. People in the local media started asking if I was just a flash in the pan. That week, a headline in one of the local papers referred to me and my day against Fred Barnett as the "Toast of Phoenix."

It was tough to have my abilities questioned like that, and I knew that my teammates were watching me to see how I would respond. Would I make excuses, or would I take responsibility for failing to make the plays I had made the year before?

As rough as the week following the Philadelphia game was, things didn't get any easier for me in the weeks that followed. My problems on the field continued the following Sunday as Dallas' Michael Irvin chalked up eight catches for 210 yards and a touchdown in the Cowboys' 31-20 win at Texas Stadium. After a week off, Washington's Gary Clark caught four balls for 106 yards. It helped that we won that game, 27-24. Two weeks later, against the New Orleans Saints, I was flagged twice for pass interference—both leading to Saints' scores—in a 30-21 loss that dropped us to 1-5.

The local papers started saying it: I was in the dreaded "sophomore slump." Many wondered how I could have regressed so much in one year, and some were saying I had become the target of our opponents' offenses because I hadn't been stopping anyone.

Although I was going through a rough time, my teammates and coaches never lost their faith in me, at least not so the public could see. They continued to support me, and many of them took some of the blame for my miseries, implying that I'd been left on my own too often. Coach Joe Bugel was my most vocal supporter, telling the papers, "I'm never worried about Aeneas Williams. He's one of hardest workers we have. He'll be fine."

Many of my teammates and coaches insisted that I was an even *better* player than I'd been the season before, that with a few breaks I'd have the same kinds of numbers I'd had in 1991.

I appreciated their support, but I also understood the cold, hard facts: I wasn't making the plays. I've always understood that football is a team game, but I also knew that if I could have made some of the plays that I'd been missing, we might have had a shot at some wins. Instead, I was lining up every week against the Fred Barnetts, the Eric Martins, and the Michael Irvins of the league and getting turned inside out.

I went through the first six games of 1992 with only three passes defensed and without an interception, and it seemed like I was getting burned more than I was making plays.

I tried not to let it bother me, but it was tough for me to take. This wasn't what I'd expected after the rookie season I'd had. I had expected to pick up right where I'd left off and continue the same kind of play I'd turned in during my first year in the league.

Fighting Back

Although I was having a tough time, I never lost confidence in what I could do. I still knew I was capable of covering the big-time receivers in the game—just like I had my rookie year.

Instead of letting my struggles rob me of my confidence, I set about solving the problems I'd been having. Where I'd worked hard in practice before, I now redoubled my efforts. I spent more time in the film room, studying what I was doing to find what was going wrong. I continued to concentrate on every play during the games and give my best physical effort. In short, I was doing everything I'd done the year before, only with extra effort.

In addition to being motivated to work harder, I did everything I could to get closer to the Lord. More than ever, I spent time in the Word and prayed. I didn't ask God to remove the test that was before me. I asked Him for strength to get through the trials and asked that He would glorify Himself through me no matter what happened.

It didn't take me long to realize that God was using this time in my football career to further mold me into the person He wanted me to be. No, God didn't cause me to get beaten on the football field, and He wasn't going to reach down and start making the plays for me, either. Those things happen as a result of my actions and the actions of my opponents. What God did do, though, was use that difficult time to get my attention and help me to grow.

God continued to drive home the things I had learned in His Word. I was going through a time where I was failing to do the things I had set out to do, the things the Cardinals paid me to do. The question now was, what would I do with the pressure? Would I use it as an excuse to quit, or would I bounce back and become a better football player and person?

You see, I had prayed that God would help me to be the best football player I could possibly be so that I could glorify Him in what I was doing. I couldn't stand the thought of going out on the field and not living up to the potential that He had put within me, and I couldn't stand the thought of selling myself short like that. Most of all, I couldn't stand the thought of not giving God the best that I had.

I knew that both God and the enemy wanted to use the pressures that were on me. God wanted to use them to help me grow in my faith and to teach me how to respond to adversity, while Satan wanted to use them to get me to make excuses for my problems, to make me feel like a failure. The enemy knew what I already knew: God wanted to use me in the lives of my teammates on the Phoenix Cardinals, and if he could get me to respond wrongly to my struggles on the football field, he could take away what God wanted to accomplish off the field.

I've always seen failure in the life of a Christian as something he or she permits. Well, I wasn't going to allow that to happen. I'd been beaten on the field—badly—but that wasn't going to make me a failure.

No Excuses!

I refused to make excuses for what had been happening to me; rather I simply acknowledged that some people had been making some big plays on me and that I had a lot to learn about playing against players of that caliber. No, I hadn't slipped on the artificial turf. I wasn't injured, and it wasn't the shoes. My opponents had simply done a great job against me.

I humbled myself before my teammates, coaches, and fans. Now it was time for God to lift me up. It was time for me to do what it took to make some plays of my own.

I was growing as a football player, but even more importantly, I was growing as a man of God. I was sinking my anchor more deeply into Him and as I did that I found that, despite the trials and tests I was going through, my confidence on the football field grew instead of being diminished, that my faith in God was strengthened instead of wavering. Finally, my play improved instead of regressing.

Ironically, I finally broke out of what was being called a "slump" in a rematch against the team we were playing when my miseries started: the Philadelphia Eagles. I finished the game, which we played at Veterans Stadium in Philadelphia, with my first interception of the year to go with three passes defensed. Our defense was outstanding that day, as the Eagles managed just nine pass completions and scored only seven points.

Unfortunately, bad breaks are a part of playing in the NFL, and we had one when I nearly scored my first NFL touchdown on my interception but tripped over a Philadelphia defender—with some inadvertent help from one of the officials—near the goal line. The Eagles then put on an impressive six-play goal-line stand—we'd gotten a new set of downs on that possession due to a penalty—to keep us out of the end zone. Unfortunately, our offense could manage just three points and we lost 7-3.

The loss to the Eagles dropped us to 1-6. Our only win up to that point was a 27-24 decision over the defending Super Bowl champion Washington Redskins, and it came as Robert Massey, my mate at cornerback, returned two interceptions for touchdowns. It came one week before the biggest win in my first two years with the Cardinals, a 24-14 victory over the eventual NFC Western Division champion San Francisco 49ers at Sun Devil Stadium.

A Badly Needed Win

The 'Niners were coming in that week with a 5-1 record and were fresh off a 56-17 demolition of the Atlanta Falcons at Candlestick Park. San Francisco had its traditionally potent offense, with quarterback Steve Young running and throwing to wide receiver Jerry Rice and tight end Brent Jones with Ricky Watters rushing and receiving.

For us, though, it was a day in which nearly everything we did worked for us.

Running back Johnny Johnson ran for 102 yards and Randall Hill caught two touchdown passes from Chris Chandler to lead our offense. Our defense that day was incredible, as we held the 49ers, the best offensive team in football that season, to less than 300 total yards offense.

We followed the win over San Francisco with our only road win of the season, 20-14 over the Los Angeles Rams at Anaheim Stadium. Again, I nearly scored my first career touchdown in the NFL. I had picked up a Ram fumble and ran sixty-one yards for what looked like the game-winning touchdown, but Eric Swann, our second year defensive tackle, was flagged for an illegal block during the runback. Fortunately for the team—and for Eric—we scored on the ensuing possession to take the win.

We lost our next four games—three of the losses were by six points or less—before getting our final win of the season, a 19-0 shutout of the New York Giants at Sun Devil Stadium in which the Giants completed only nine of their twenty-five passes.

One of our losses—the 16-10 decision to the eventual Super Bowl champion Dallas Cowboys at Sun Devil Stadium—was especially hard to take because we'd led for much of the game. I made a diving interception, then got up and ran seventy-eight yards to the end zone for what looked like a touchdown—again, it would have been my first—and a 14-3 Cardinals lead. Unfortunately for us, one of the officials ruled that I had been downed by contact after the interception, and the touchdown was called back.

A Great—But Tough—Year

As far as the record is concerned, the Phoenix Cardinals had a tough season in 1992, finishing 4-12 and in last place in the NFC Eastern Division. That year we lost six games by one touchdown or less.

I finished the season with forty-eight solo tackles and three interceptions—half the number I'd posted in 1991. While my numbers might have been down from the previous year, it was a great year for me. It was a year where I grew more as a player and as a person than any year before.

I'm not going to tell you it wasn't tough to go through the struggles I did during the first part of the year. It was tough, and I'd never wish something like that on anybody. But I appreciate what I went through, because it made me stronger and more determined to make submitting myself to God my top priority on the football field.

I continued to work out hard during the offseason—remember, too, that I also got married in February of that year—and my relationship with the Lord continued to strengthen and grow.

God continued to rain blessings down on me in every area of my life. One of those blessings came in the form of a man who helped me to become the football player I am today.

Submitting to a Mentor

Gill Byrd wasn't the fastest cornerback in the National Football League. He wasn't the quickest and he wasn't the hardest hitter.

What he was, though, was one of the best. In addition to his excellent coverage of receivers, he'd had thirty-one interceptions over the five seasons from 1988–92. He'd been picked for his second straight Pro Bowl after the '92 season.

We hosted Gill Byrd's team, the San Diego Chargers, late in the 1992 season. We hadn't played San Diego the previous season or in the preseason, so it was the first time I'd seen him play up close and in person.

I was impressed with how smart of a football player Gill was. He was considered "slow" by NFL cornerback standards, but his technique was flawless and he was rarely beaten. He was one of the best I have ever seen play. He played a position in the NFL where it's said you need superhuman speed, and he played it as well as anybody. In one afternoon, I grew to admire Gill Byrd, and I wanted to know if he would teach me any of the things he knew.

I had a chance to meet Gill after the game. We talked for a short time, and before we left the field, I said, "I'm going to call you this offseason."

Gill never expected me to call, but I did.

"I'd like to get together with you and ask you some questions about how you play the game," I said. "I want to learn how you do it."

You don't find a lot of players in the NFL—particularly from opposing teams—who are willing to take a less-experienced player under their wing and teach them the things they need to know to get better. Everyone has their own little "turf" to protect, and they don't want to give away their secrets.

You also don't find a lot of young players in the NFL who will ask questions and allow an older player to help them out. Most of them don't like to ask questions of veterans like that, fearing that they'll come off looking like they don't know anything. I've never taken that approach, though.

I've always tried to operate by the verse that says, "Seek and you will find," and I always ask questions when I'm around other players, particularly players who have more experience than I do. I'd done the same thing following my first season when I met Kenny Houston, the Hall of Fame defensive back who played for the Houston Oilers. I met Kenny at the NFL Players Association awards banquet that year, and I asked him questions about how to improve myself as a football player. Kenny Houston, himself a Christian man, opened his heart to me and invited me to come to Houston, Texas, to visit with him. I did, and he taught me a lot about playing cornerback in the NFL. Kenny works at a high school in Houston, and I went to the school and worked out with him—during a physical education class, no less.

I wanted to talk to Kenny Houston because he had information that I didn't yet possess. It was the same with Gill Byrd. I wanted to know what he knew.

Gill graciously said he'd be happy to meet with me, and we arranged a time for a visit. I couldn't wait to meet with him.

Off to San Diego

Tracy and I, still newlyweds at the time, flew to San Diego, and we found Gill Byrd and his wife, Marilyn—a Christian couple themselves—to be a couple who truly had the gift of hospitality. They welcomed us into their home and made us feel completely welcome.

Later that day, it was time for me to submit myself to the teaching of someone I considered a master of our craft.

Gill took me to the San Diego Chargers' practice facility, where he taught me things about playing cornerback that I had no idea existed, or if I did know they existed, I didn't have any idea how to do them as well as he did. He taught me how to backpedal, how to break on the ball, how to plant at the right moment. He showed me step by step how to do those things, then watched while I tried to imitate what he'd done. He encouraged me and challenged me as I worked, stopping me and correcting me when I needed it.

Gill and I also talked about the mental aspect of the game. He taught me how to better use my mind on the football field. He taught me how to analyze the game and break it down. He talked to me about studying positions, reading quarterbacks, and training. That season, he took time out of his busy schedule and flew to Phoenix and went with me to the Cardinals film room to help me learn to study film.

I'm still grateful to Gill Byrd for the help he gave me, and I'm grateful to the Lord for bringing him into my life. He played as big a role as any man in helping me become the player I've become. He not only taught me a lot about playing cornerback in the NFL, but he also taught me a lot about being a husband and father. As I observed him with his wife and children, I realized that his was the kind of family I wanted to have. He was a source of encouragement and an example to me of what a husband and father should be, and that was exactly what I needed at the time.

As I headed into the 1993 season—and into the first few years of my marriage—I was eager to use the things that Gill Byrd had taught me.

Early Struggles in '93

Heading into the 1993 season, there was reason to believe that there would be major improvements for the Phoenix Cardinals. We'd finished strong on defense in 1992, and with the continued maturation of players such as linemen Eric Swann, Michael Bankston, Keith Rucker, and Rueben Davis as well as the play of linebackers Eric Hill and Freddie Joe Nunn, it appeared we would continue to improve.

The Cardinals had drafted to upgrade the offense in 1993, using their top pick—the third pick overall—to take University of Georgia running back Garrison Hearst. In addition, they nabbed offensive tackles Ernest Dye of South Carolina and Ben Coleman of Wake Forest. Both players weighed more than 310 pounds and were considered potential starters as rookies.

The Cardinals were a team with some potential. The only question was whether that potential would translate into wins. Maybe training camp was something of a harbinger of things to come. First of all, Garrison Hearst got caught in a contract dispute with the team and missed all of the preseason. It's never good news when a team's prized rookie isn't in camp with the rest of the team, and it wasn't good news for us when Garrison held out.

The 1993 season started for the Phoenix Cardinals pretty much like the 1992 season had: slowly. At the halfway point of the season we were sitting at a not-too-pretty 2-6, which was exactly what our record was the previous year. There were some heart-breaking losses along the way, too, as all but one of our losses came by one touchdown or less. We were so close to a winning record that we could taste it, yet we always found a way to lose.

It was a time of adversity for me and my teammates. Each week, we came out believing we could win, but each week we walked off the field with another close loss. We wondered what we needed to do to get it right.

It was frustrating for me to lose all those games, especially when we were so close to winning most of them. I believed at the time—and I still do—that there was something to be learned in those losses and that they would make me and my teammates better players and better people if we allowed that to happen. At the same time, though, I wanted to win, and I continued to do all I could to make that a reality.

In doing that, it was at the halfway point of the season that I had what was up to that point the highlight of my NFL career.

Hitting Paydirt—Twice

Despite my team's losing record, I was growing in confidence and in my reputation as an NFL cornerback as the 1993 season wore on. I found that teams weren't trying to pick on me as much, but since I always covered receivers like Jerry Rice and Michael Irvin during our games, I saw the ball plenty. I saw it enough, in fact, that I had a highlight game that season.

In what is still a memorable game for me, I scored the first two touchdowns of my career. What made it all the sweeter was that it was against my hometown team—the New Orleans Saints. It was sweet because I knew that the game would be televised from Sun Devil Stadium to the New Orleans area—just as my game against Fred Barnett and the Philadelphia Eagles had been the season before. That would give my hometown a chance to see what I could do.

We were trailing the Saints 7-3 when I scored my first touchdown—on a fumble recovery. Greg Davis had just kicked a 28-yard field goal in the first quarter for our first points of the day. After a procedure penalty, the Saints offense came to the line of scrimmage for a first-and-15 play from their own

15-yard line. New Orleans quarterback Wade Wilson threw a 5-yard pass to Quinn Early, but Robert Massey—my partner at the right cornerback position—delivered a hit that separated Early from the ball. When I realized Early had fumbled, I raced over, picked up the ball, and ran twenty yards up the left sideline for my first NFL touchdown. At that point, we led 10-7.

I was and am grateful to God for the touchdown, but I still have to give Robert Massey—who played for the Saints in 1989–90—all the credit. He made a great play to jar the ball loose from Early's hands, and all I had to do was pick it up and run it in. It might have been the easiest touchdown in the NFL that season. I later told the local papers, "A kid could have gotten the ball and run it in." I believed it then, and I believe it now.

I wasn't done that day, though. I had another personal highlight coming—my first NFL touchdown on an interception return.

That touchdown came late in the second quarter when I stepped in front of Saints receiver Eric Martin and picked off a pass from Wilson. I could see Wilson looking Martin's way, and I knew what he wanted to do. I baited him into throwing the ball to my area by making him think I was going one direction when I was going the other. He fell for the bait, and he threw the ball toward Martin. I knew it was coming, and it was just a matter of hanging onto the ball to get the interception.

With my first interception of the season tucked under my arm, I raced down the right sideline, then cut back to elude a diving tackle attempt by Wilson. I then picked up a block from Eric Swann and ran into the end zone for a 46-yard return. We led 17-7 at that point—with just over five minutes left in the half—and it looked like we were on our way to our third win of the season.

Unfortunately, we didn't score another point and wound up losing 20-17. That was probably the most bittersweet day any player in the NFL has ever had. I was thrilled that I'd scored two touchdowns, but I was also deeply disappointed that we'd lost. During the game, I had tried to block out of my mind the fact that I was playing my hometown team, but I wanted to win that game more than anything.

I loved scoring the touchdowns, but I hated losing. All I could do was continue to work hard in practice and in the games and hope that the wins would come. As it turns out, it would be sooner rather than later that the Cardinals would enjoy some long-awaited on-field success.

Finishing Strong

One week after the New Orleans game, we got our third win of the season, beating the Philadelphia Eagles 16-3 at Sun Devil Stadium. I then had my second interception of the season, returning the ball 41 yards to set up our only touchdown.

After losing two more close games—20-15 in Dallas and 19-17 against the New York Giants—something happened to the Cardinals. We started playing some of the best football we'd played in my three seasons with the team, winning three of our last four to finish 7-9, the team's best season since 1988.

We'd fallen short in our bid for a winning record, but the way we finished the season was encouraging to us. It was a foundation on which to build for the following season.

Although I had just two interceptions in 1993, it was a good season for me and for the rest of the Cardinal defense. Despite finishing twenty-first in the league in total defense, we had finished eighth where it counts: in points allowed. In addition, the team had finished eighth in the league in total offense. For the first time in nine seasons, the Cardinals had scored more points than they had given up (326-269).

But all those numbers don't mean a thing if you aren't winning. The bottom line in the National Football League is wins and losses, and team owner Bill Bidwell decided it was time for a coaching change. He fired Coach Joe Bugel—who had a record of 20-44 in his three seasons with the team—and brought in a coach that almost nobody would have expected to be his choice to lead the Cardinals.

It was time for a new era for the Cardinals. The only question for me, though, was would I be a part of it.

PASS COVERAGE

1. Do you set goals for yourself? If so, what criteria do you use to set those goals?

2. Have you ever been embarrassed in front of people by what you considered a personal failure? How did you respond?

3. Do you tend to lose confidence in what God is doing in your life when you face adversity or do you remain confident? What are some examples of that in your life?

4. How important do you think winning is to God? Why is the effort to succeed important to Him?

CHAPTER EIGHT

A SEASON OF CHANGE

GETTING ACCUSTOMED TO "BUDDY BALL"

"But your hearts must be fully committed to the LORD our God,
to live by his decrees and obey his commands, as at this time."

—1 KINGS 8:61

The 1994 National Football League season brought big changes for the Cardinals, starting with their name. In March of that year—four months before training camp—the NFL owners unanimously approved team owner Bill Bidwell's request to rename the team the "Arizona Cardinals."

The name change, however, paled in importance to what had happened to the coaching staff. Despite our strong finish in 1993, Bill Bidwell fired Coach Joe Bugel, the only head coach I'd known since I came into the league, then surprised just about every observer by hiring Buddy Ryan as the team's head coach and general manager.

Let Me Outta Here!

A lot of the Cardinals players were skeptical about Coach Ryan, but most of them said they would give the man a chance. After all, most of his former players spoke very well of him, and he'd had a lot of success as an NFL coach. I, too, was skeptical, but I wasn't so sure I wanted to give him a chance. In fact, at first I said I didn't want to play for him.

"There's no way I'm going to stay here and play for Coach Ryan," I told Tracy when I found out that the team had hired him.

I told Tracy about the stories I'd heard about Coach Ryan, that he was seen as a taskmaster and a "my way or the highway" kind of coach. I'd heard that he was a coach who had some unorthodox ways about him, that he had a way of saying controversial things in the media and to his players. I knew there must have been something to those stories, especially after I—along with everyone else in the country with even the most casual interest in football—had seen the incident on the sidelines of a Houston Oilers game the previous season, when Coach Ryan, then the Oilers' defensive coordinator, took a punch at Kevin Gilbride, Houston's offensive coordinator, during an argument.

I couldn't argue with what Coach Ryan had accomplished in his NFL coaching career, though. I knew that he was the architect of the famed "46" defense that was as responsible as anything for the Chicago Bears' devastating 15-1 season in 1985 and their dominating run through the playoffs that year, including the 46-10 Super Bowl XX rout of the New England Patriots. I knew he'd taken over a mediocre Philadelphia Eagles team the following season and within a few years guided it into the playoffs. I knew he'd built a high-quality defense when he was with the Oilers. Obviously, he had some solid coaching credentials.

Still, I didn't want to play for Coach Ryan. As I had told Tracy, I didn't want to deal with the way he operated. I wanted to go somewhere else, and there was a chance that season I could do just that.

Having completed my third year in the league, I was what is called a restricted free agent, meaning that if I signed with another club the Cardinals had the right to match the offer and keep me. If I'd had four years' experience at that time, I would have been an unrestricted free agent, meaning I could have signed with anyone, and the Cardinals would have had no rights to match the offer.

I wanted to sign with another team and hope—maybe even ask—that the Cardinals didn't try to match the offer.

Something funny happened on the way to my leaving the Arizona Cardinals, though. God said, "No." He also showed me that I wasn't being honest with myself about my reasons for wanting to leave.

What I Was *Really* Thinking

It always amazes me how God looks at what's truly in our hearts and not as much at what we're saying. He has a way of cutting through everything we say and getting to the real issue. He did that to me prior to the 1994 NFL season.

I had been telling myself and my wife that I didn't want to deal with Coach Ryan because of his personality and coaching style, but that wasn't the problem at all. I knew I could deal with Coach Ryan. I'd played for tough coaches before, and I knew I could handle anything Coach Ryan threw my way.

What I didn't know if I could deal with was his defensive system, which calls for a lot of strictly man-to-man coverage on the receivers by the cornerbacks. It's what is called putting the cornerback on an "island."

I had spent three years playing in Coach Joe Bugel's defensive system, which was more zone oriented. I still matched up with the great receivers, but I knew there would be some help if I was beaten. Now I was looking at the possibility of playing in a system where I would be covering guys like Cris Carter, Michael Irvin, and Irving Fryar all by myself. Even with help, it was tough enough staying with those guys, but I couldn't see myself doing it strictly man to man. I had visions of the first game against Philadelphia in 1992 becoming the rule, rather than the exception in my career.

Basically, God pointed out that I wasn't worried about Coach Ryan, but that I was, in a word, afraid. I wasn't dealing with an irrational fear. I had some legitimate, rational concerns about my ability to do what I knew Coach Ryan would ask of me. I had nothing personal against Coach Ryan; in fact, I respected what he had accomplished in the league. But I knew he would be asking me to make some tremendous changes in the way I played my position, and I honestly didn't know if I was capable of doing it.

When I told Tracy that I didn't want to play for Coach Ryan, I was like someone who says he won't go out on a boat because he's afraid of the water. If you were to ask that same man if he showers in water, has water in his swimming pool, or drinks water, he'll say yes. The truth of the matter, then, is that he isn't afraid of water. That's an irrational fear, because he's around water every day. What he's really afraid of is dying. He's afraid of drowning. That's a rational fear.

Like that man who said he was afraid of water, I had to look in the mirror and ask myself what I was really afraid of. I had to figure out what was really going on inside me. I had to ask myself if I had the courage to step out of my comfort zone—in this case, the kind of defense that Coach Bugel employed—and try something new and different.

What Does God Want?

When I told Tracy that I didn't want to play for Coach Ryan, she asked me the question that I needed to hear: "Have you prayed about it?"

As we prayed about my decision, it became clear to both of us that God wasn't done with me in Phoenix yet, that I was to go forward and resign with the Cardinals—if they wanted me.

They did. I signed a two-year contract with the Arizona Cardinals and got ready for my fourth season in the National Football League. I felt a lot of apprehension about playing in Coach Buddy Ryan's system, but I was ready and willing to go forward and submit myself to what my new boss wanted me to do.

A New Look

I'll never forget what Robert Ryan—the Cardinals defensive back's coach and son of the head coach—said to me the first day of our 1994 minicamp. "I've seen you play in college and in the NFL, and there's no reason why you can't lead the NFL in interceptions every year."

It was just the kind of encouragement I needed, right when I needed it. I thanked Robert Ryan for the compliment, then thanked God for what the man had said to me, because it affirmed to me that I was right where I belonged.

I had a strong minicamp, and I left feeling encouraged about the upcoming season. I believed that God was going to bless me because of my willingness to stay where He wanted me, but I had no idea what great things were going to be happening to me that year.

I came into training camp in shape and ready to play, but still wondering how I'd adjust to playing in Coach Buddy Ryan's defensive system.

How Did I Play, You Ask?

I had the best training camp I'd had up to that point. Instead of feeling nervous or afraid of making mistakes while playing in the new system, I met the challenge of stepping out of that three-year comfort zone head on. Coach Ryan's defensive system was one that can destroy a young cornerback's confidence, but I wasn't going to let that happen. I had decided that if Coach Ryan wanted me to cover receivers one on one, then I was going to do it the best I possibly could.

In practice and in the preseason games, I was covering people, making plays, and getting my coaches' attention. It was around that time that Coach Ryan started telling everybody who would listen that I was one of the elite cornerbacks—in the same class as Deion Sanders—in the NFL.

Coach Buddy Ryan got in front of the media one day that preseason and said, "Aeneas Williams may be the best cornerback I've ever been around, and I've been around quite a few great corners. This guy's going to be in Hawaii at the Pro Bowl at the end of the season."

This from a man who had coached some of the great cornerbacks ever to put on an NFL uniform. He'd coached Eric Allen when he was with the Eagles, Cris Dishman and Darryll Lewis at Houston, and Leslie Frazier with the Super Bowl champion Bears.

As much as I enjoyed hearing what Coach Ryan was saying about me, I didn't know if I totally agreed with him. I was confident in my own abilities, but I didn't know if I was in the same class as the elite cornerbacks.

What I soon found out, however, was that Coach Ryan's words changed how I was perceived. Prior to that season, I had been seen as a solid, steady player, but now my coach—who was considered one of the great defensive coaches in the game—was talking about me like I was a Pro Bowl player.

When the season started, I wasn't on the field making a conscious effort to make the Pro Bowl or to lead the league in interceptions. I was just trying to play the best football I could and letting whatever honors I was to receive come my way.

They did!

Moving Up

We made some big strides during Coach Buddy Ryan's first year with the Arizona Cardinals. We finished 8-8 for the team's first nonlosing record since 1984. But it wasn't before we endured a tough start to the season.

The Cardinals started out 0-2 with two close losses—14-12 to the Los Angeles Rams at Anaheim Stadium and 20-17 to the New York Giants at Sun Devil Stadium—before being blown out 32-0 by the Cleveland Browns in Cleveland to go 0-3.

We went 3-3 through the next six weeks of the season to go 3-6 overall, before winning five of our last seven games. We had a chance for a winning season, but we lost 10-6 to the Falcons at Atlanta to finish the season at 8-8.

It was an encouraging season for the team, and I was grateful to God to be a part of it. But as much as I felt blessed by the success of the team, I was in awe of what God had done in my career that season.

We got our first win of the season by beating the Minnesota Vikings 17-7 at Sun Devil Stadium. I spent the day covering Cris Carter, and I had one interception. Two weeks later, James Williams—my mate at cornerback—and I each had two interceptions as we beat the Washington Redskins 19-16 in overtime at RFK Stadium. It was a memorable game in which one of my interceptions set up a Cardinal touchdown and another stopped a Redskin scoring drive at our 16-yard line. I also recovered a blocked field goal attempt in the overtime to help give the team a chance to win. The effort got me some personal recognition, too, as I was named the National Football Conference defensive player of the week.

Later that season, I had a game that many people thought was my best of the year in the Cardinals' 12-6 win over the Philadelphia Eagles. I was assigned to cover Fred Barnett, the Eagles' big-play receiver who had burned us for eleven catches for 173 yards and two touchdowns in a 17-7 Philadelphia win earlier in the season. I wasn't looking at the matchup with Fred as a chance for revenge or a chance to redeem myself. Fred had had some big games against the Cardinals and against me. (Remember the eight-catch, two-touchdown game against me early in my second season?) It was a challenge to me to try to stop one of the top receivers in the game at that time. I took that challenge very seriously.

I knew that if I wasn't at my best, I could be in for a long day against Fred Barnett. He was having his best season as a pro and one of the best seasons of any wide receiver that year. I covered Fred man-to-man all day, and when the game was over he'd recorded four catches for just twenty-four yards. In addition, I had an interception at the goal line to stop an Eagle drive and a recovery of a fumble by Herschel Walker in Arizona territory to stop another drive.

By the time the season ended, I had tied for the league lead in interceptions—with Cleveland Browns' safety Eric Turner—with nine, the most by a Cardinal since Hall of Fame Larry Wilson recorded ten in 1966. In addition, I'd recorded a career high of sixteen pass deflections and what is still a career high of twenty-eight passes defensed.

It was a good time on the field for me and my teammates, but there was more to it than that. In addition to our growth as football players, we also grew as men.

A Time for Growth

The 1994 season wasn't just a time when the Arizona Cardinals began to receive respect as a football team, but a time when there was tremendous spiritual growth for many of us on the team and a time when God allowed me to publicly give Him the glory for my success on the field.

I'm still amazed when I think about it, but that season was the start of a time when men on our team were coming into a relationship with the Lord, when guys who had known Him but were drifting spiritually drew closer to

Him, and a time when we all grew in our knowledge of the Word of God. There was a hunger for the Word of God on the team, and the Lord elevated me in the midst of the team and allowed me to start teaching my teammates the Word.

God also allowed me to grow in stature in the eyes of my teammates. I found myself spending incredible amounts of time encouraging and exhorting my teammates to be more bold in proclaiming their faith and in living the kinds of lives they knew God wanted them to live. It was incredible to see the hunger that God was putting in the hearts of these men for His Word and to know Him better.

It started at the beginning of training camp, when we started having Bible Studies and prayer meetings every night until curfew. Every night we had no fewer than twenty guys taking part in the Bible Study. We used this time to encourage one another in our faith and build one another up in the knowledge of the Word of God.

That season I was able more than ever to give God glory for the way He had blessed my career. Because of the season I was having, members of the media—in Phoenix and around the nation—flocked around me and wanted to know what I was doing to have such a good season.

I was granted an extra dose of courage when I was able to share my faith more boldly than I ever had before. And the courage that God gave me was contagious, too, as other guys on the team started reaching out in more boldness. They saw my boldness and that helped give them the courage that they had lacked. Guys were going from being quiet, closet believers to being bold spokesmen for the faith.

Tracy was seeing the same kind of victory in her ministry. She led—and still leads—a Bible study and prayer meeting for the players' wives, and she started to see the same kind of growth in the women that I was seeing in the men.

It was amazing to me how the more I lifted up the Lord Jesus Christ the more He lifted me up in the eyes of the world. As the season wore on, I started to get more and more attention from the media, mostly because of the way I was playing that season.

I'm not going to lie to you: I enjoyed the attention. But more than that, I enjoyed the opportunity to take that attention and deflect it toward the One who made it all possible. I told the reporters that God had placed in me the "spirit of excellence," and that He had done that so that I could glorify Him on the football field. I told them that my goal all that season was to play for the Lord and please Him and that in doing that I had pleased the people who came to see me and my teammates play.

It's amazing to think about how God used Coach Buddy Ryan both to encourage me and to promote me early in the season and how that promotion helped lift me up so that I could glorify God in what I was doing.

It was also amazing how everything Coach Ryan and his son had said about me early that season came to pass. I led the league in interceptions and played as well as any cornerback, just like they'd said.

There was one more thing Coach Ryan had said would happen to me, something about a trip to Hawaii when the season was over.

On to the Pro Bowl?

Late that season, I thought a lot about the possibility of going to the Pro Bowl. Although I didn't dwell on it, it was always in the back of my mind. I knew I'd had my best year in the pros and that I'd played just about as well as any cornerback in the NFL that season, but I still didn't know if I had a shot at the Pro Bowl.

I remember looking around the Cardinals' locker room late that season and seeing the words "Pro Bowl" stenciled in next to the names of some of my teammates who had been selected in previous years. It made me wonder what it's like to go to the Pro Bowl, and it made me wonder when and if I would be honored that way.

I wanted to be selected, but I also knew that the decision was ultimately up to the players, coaches, and fans. They—not me—were the ones who would determine if I deserved to go. The way I saw it, I'd already been blessed just to play in the NFL and nobody owed me a thing. If they thought I'd played well enough that season to go to the Pro Bowl, I'd go. If not, I wasn't going to feel slighted, and I'd have something to shoot for the next season.

The Word of God says that God makes all things happen in His time, and the 1994 season was His time to honor me as a member of the National Football Conference Pro Bowl team.

I first found out that I'd been selected for the Pro Bowl when a reporter from one of the Phoenix papers walked up to me as I was finishing practice and said, "Congratulations! You've been selected as a starter in the Pro Bowl."

I was one of two Cardinals players to be selected to the Pro Bowl. The other, linebacker Seth Joyner, was named as a reserve. Fullback Larry Centers and defensive tackle Eric Swann were named first alternates, meaning if someone in their position had to pull out of the game, they would take his place. Linebacker Eric Hill was a second alternate.

Even though I was hearing it from someone who would know, I still had a hard time believing it. I thought about the guys I had played with in high school and college and how I felt that they were far more talented than I was, yet here I was, selected for my first Pro Bowl.

I'm not one to be overly demonstrative when I'm excited or happy about something, but I felt a wave of gratitude come over me for the honor I had received. It was—and still is—gratifying to be recognized for something you work so hard to achieve. It's gratifying because you know that your coaches, peers, and fans respect what you do and how well you do it.

I looked at the reporter and simply said, "Thank you," then told him how much I appreciated the help I'd received from Coach Ryan and his staff. I couldn't have been more sincere, either. I was grateful for how Coach Ryan took the time early in the season to put my name in the public's eye, how he compared me with some of the great cornerbacks he'd coached during his coaching career.

More than that, though, I was grateful to my Lord for allowing me to have the kind of year I'd had and for allowing me to give Him the glory for what had happened to me that season. I knew that God didn't have to allow me to be a Pro Bowl player, and that made it all the sweeter that He had.

After I got the news, I could hardly wait to tell my wife. I'll never forget her reaction when I told her. I was just as excited as she was that I was going, but she was the one whose excitement showed the most. Next I called Mom and Dad to tell them. I knew they'd be pleased; after all, they had a personal stake in me going to the Pro Bowl that went beyond the fact that I was their son and that they would be proud of me.

Off to the Pro Bowl

Tracy and I headed to Honolulu for the Pro Bowl, and we were anything but alone. You see, it was a given to me—and to my family—that Mom and Dad would be going with us. In fact, I brought every member of the family who wanted to go, including my brothers, my aunts and uncles, my in-laws. I don't remember exactly how many people came with us for my first Pro Bowl, but suffice it to say that my family alone gave the Hawaii tourist industry quite a boost that week.

While I was honored and excited to be going to my first Pro Bowl, it was a time of adjustment for me. I'd spent all season working as hard as I could to get there, and once I was there I found it to be the most laid-back, relaxed placed I'd ever visited. It was a culture shock for me, to say the least.

One of the things about the Pro Bowl that's a little hard to adjust to at first is that you are now teammates with guys you've tried to beat all season long. In fact, one of my biggest rivals—wide receiver Cris Carter of the Minnesota Vikings—became not just a friend during Pro Bowl week, but a partner in leading a Bible study for the players who wanted to come.

During practice for the Pro Bowl, the players jog through a few basics in preparation for the game. Most of the guys were still in good shape after having played football the previous six months, but some were still nursing bumps and bruises from the season.

Although the game itself isn't a full-speed affair—most of the time the players go about three-quarters speed until the last few possessions—I still found myself working as hard as I could to keep the people I was covering from catching a pass. I knew it didn't really count for anything and that people usually don't even remember who won the game, but I still wanted to play my best when I was out there. I hate it when my man catches a pass, and that includes when it happens in the Pro Bowl.

Submitting by Overcoming Fear

My first appearance in the Pro Bowl was a great ending to a great season in which God showed me what can happen when I face up to the fears that could, if I allowed them to, drag me down to mediocrity, both in my relationship with Him and as a football player.

I came very close to saying no to the challenge that was before me when the 1994 season started. God had other plans, though. He still had work for me to do in Arizona, and He wasn't going to let me run away from the Cardinals with my tail between my legs.

Playing in Coach Ryan's system turned out to be just as challenging as I thought it would be, but it took me out of my comfort zone and allowed the potential that was already in me to come out.

God rewarded my decision to submit to His will—and to Coach Ryan's defensive philosophy—and stay with the Arizona Cardinals. He did that by helping me to establish myself as one of the top defensive players in the NFL that season. But there was more. He also put me in a position of respect before my teammates, the very people He called me to Phoenix to minister to.

It also appeared that the 1994 season just might be a springboard for further success for the Arizona Cardinals. The only question was, could we pick up from where we'd left off?

PASS COVERAGE

1. How do you respond to change in your life?

2. Have you ever wanted to run away from a situation simply because there were changes that made you uncomfortable?

3. How important is it to you to give God glory when you are put in a position of prominence?

4. Is it important to you to have the respect of your peers at school or work? Why or why not?

CHAPTER NINE

◄ HOPE SPRINGS ETERNAL ►

BUILDING A WINNER IN ARIZONA

With God we will gain the victory,
and he will trample down our enemies.

—PSALM 60:12

The new-look Arizona Cardinals—the same Cardinals who had shown so much promise during the 1994 season under Coach Buddy Ryan—took several steps backwards in 1995 in their bid to finally field a winning football team for their longsuffering fans.

We didn't play well on offense, and we didn't play well on defense. Statistically, we were at or near the bottom of the league standings in just about every major category. We'd had an outstanding year on defense in 1994, finishing third in total defense, but we couldn't stop anybody in 1995. We gave up more points than any other team in the league. We weren't much better on offense. Only two teams—the expansion Jacksonville Jaguars and the Tampa Bay Buccaneers—scored fewer points than we did.

We won just four games in 1995, and only one of those came against a team with a winning record. We had three different three-game losing streaks, and a lot of people thought we were fortunate to win four games.

It was, to say the least, a trying season for everybody involved.

Letting the Light Shine

In the midst of a difficult season for the Cardinals, God still blessed me personally with a good season. I pulled in six more interceptions, returning two of those for touchdowns. I was named for the second consecutive year as a starter in the Pro Bowl. In addition, I was named All-Pro by the Associated Press, *College and Pro Football Newsweekly, Pro Football Weekly, The Sporting News, USA Today,* and the Pro Football Writers Association.

Although I appreciated the personal honors, I still wanted to win. At the same time, though, I still submitted myself to accomplishing the purpose for which I knew God had sent me to Arizona: to draw people to Himself.

While it was tough dealing with losing, it was still a time of growth for me and my teammates. Yes, we had some of the internal team problems that come from a frustrating season, but at the same time there was a lot of spiritual and personal growth going on with the Arizona Cardinals.

Again, it was a time when God gave me the opportunity to give him glory, and also a time when He was able to glorify Himself through me before our fans by healing me of the effects of an injury I received in our fourth game of the season, against the Dallas Cowboys at Texas Stadium.

I was running to make a tackle on Emmitt Smith but held up when he crossed the goal line for a touchdown in the second quarter. When I planted my foot to stop my left knee gave way, and I went crashing to the turf, clutching my knee in agony. The Cardinals' crew of medical personnel and trainers rushed out on the field to check me out, then helped me to the sideline. My day was over. I returned to the game in the second half, only to stand on the sidelines leaning on a pair of crutches as the Cowboys finished their 34-20 win.

Initially, the doctors said I'd probably be out two to three weeks with a sprained knee and that I certainly wouldn't be playing the following week in our home game against the Kansas City Chiefs. I wasn't buying that, though. I knew that God was going to heal the knee, and I said so to the Phoenix media. I told the skeptical listeners that I wouldn't miss a game with the injury.

I didn't, either. Although nobody really believed I could play, I was practicing by the middle of that week. I still felt a little sore and there was some water on the knee, but the team doctor could find no structural damage. With God's help, I was able to play against the Chiefs.

Unfortunately, we lost 24-3 to go 1-4. Things didn't get much better during the next eleven games, and when the season ended, so did Coach Buddy Ryan's tenure with the Cardinals. It was time for another change in direction.

A New Direction

The head coach is often the first casualty of a losing season in the NFL, and Coach Buddy Ryan wasn't an exception to that rule. With our 4-12 season in 1995 behind us, team owner Bill Bidwell let Coach Ryan and his staff of assistants go and brought in Vince Tobin to rebuild the team.

There would be big changes coming for the Cardinals in 1996, but once again I wasn't sure at that point if I would be a part of those changes. I was an unrestricted free agent at the end of the '95 season, and I was considering some offers I was receiving from other teams. But I also was strongly considering resigning with the Cardinals.

There were several factors I was looking at as I thought about what I would do. I thought about the ministry I'd had with my teammates and whether God wanted me to return. I also thought about the direction the team was headed and whether Coach Tobin would be a good man to take the Cardinals there.

In addition to praying about these things and giving them hours and hours of thought, I did some research on the Cardinals new coach. I knew he had an excellent reputation as a defensive coach and that he'd done an outstanding job as the Indianapolis Colts' defensive coordinator the previous two years. I'd also heard good things about him from some of his players, including my friends Eugene Daniel and Ashley Ambrose (remember, Ashley was a friend and teammate of mine from high school), both cornerbacks with the Colts under Coach Tobin.

I found out that Coach Tobin is a man who puts a great deal of emphasis on character—that he's a man with character, and he hires people with character. From everything I could see, that was true. Right away, he hired a quality staff full of experienced, quality coaches, including former Arizona State University head coach Larry Marmie and longtime NFL assistant Dave McGinnis. In addition, he hired Mean Joe Greene, the Hall of Fame defensive tackle on the four-time Super Bowl champion Pittsburgh Steelers of the 1970s, as his defensive line coach. (Now there's a man who knows something about winning!)

I liked what I heard about Coach Tobin and I liked what I was seeing, and I knew the team would be in good hands with him as the head coach.

Not long into the free-agent signing season, I signed a five-year contract with the Cardinals.

A New Outlook

Even though we'd endured a tough season in 1995, I and all my Cardinals teammates came into the 1996 campaign feeling optimistic. We truly believed we had a chance to be a winner.

Coach Tobin was doing everything he could to bring improvements to the Cardinals. Garrison Hearst, the former first-round draft pick of the Cardinals and a 1,000-yard rusher in 1995, was gone to the Cincinnati Bengals, but Coach Tobin had stepped in and made some bold moves in the free agent market, including signing six-time Pro Bowl offensive tackle Lomas Brown from the Lions and veteran quarterback Boomer Esiason from the New York Jets. In addition, the Cardinals drafted a pass rushing ace in All-American defensive end Simeon Rice of Illinois.

It seemed like things were going to get better for us.

We improved right away, too, but it was hard for anybody to see during our first three games—all losses, two of which weren't close.

The local media were starting to wonder if we were moving backward instead of forward from the 1995 season. Here we were, starting out 0-3 and getting completely dominated along the way.

We finally broke into the win column with a 28-14 win over the Saints in my hometown of New Orleans. LeShon Johnson, our second-year running back from Northern Illinois, had a franchise-record 214 yards rushing and two touchdowns—both in the fourth quarter—to lead us to the win.

We split our next four games to go 3-5 during the first half of the season, then lost 16-8 to the New York Giants at Giants Stadium. We finally got to

.500 on the season with three wins in a row—over the Washington Redskins at RFK Stadium and over the New York Giants and the Philadelphia Eagles at Sun Devil Stadium. Those three wins in a row gave us a 6-6 record heading into the final quarter of the season and gave the team its first winning November since 1986.

The win over the Redskins—37-34 in overtime—featured a record-setting performance by Boomer Esiason, who completed 35 of 59 passing for a team record 522 yards and three touchdowns, two of which came in the fourth quarter to help get the game into overtime. Obviously, it wasn't a game with a lot of defensive highlights, but I had a good game against Henry Ellard, holding him to one reception for nineteen yards.

A week later we beat the Giants 31-24. I had my fourth interception of the year, setting up a Kevin Butler field goal in the fourth quarter.

We beat the Eagles 36-30 to complete our winning streak. Boomer Esiason had his third outstanding game in a row, passing for 340 yards and two touchdowns, including a 24-yarder to Marcus Dowdell with fourteen seconds left in the game to put us ahead.

With a 6-6 record after twelve games, the Cardinals were excited at the possibility of closing out the 1996 season with a winning record and a possible playoff berth. Unfortunately, we finished out the season by losing three of our final four to go 7-9.

Personally, I'd had a good season, pulling in six interceptions for the second year in a row and being named a starter in the Pro Bowl and first-team All-Pro. I was happy with how I played, and I looked forward to what we could accomplish in the coming year.

Taking the Next Step?

There was a feeling of optimism heading into the 1997 season that I hadn't seen before with the Cardinals. We had pulled together as a team like never before, and we believed we had a legitimate chance to be in the playoffs.

Our defense—which featured some impressive players such as Simeon Rice, the NFL Defensive Rookie of the Year after recording twelve and a half sacks in 1996; Eric Swann, a Pro Bowl player from 1996; middle linebacker Eric Hill, who led the team with 196 tackles; and strong safety Matt Darby.

On offense, Kent Graham, our starting quarterback after Boomer Esiason had been released, seemed to be coming into his own, and fullback Larry Centers was coming off a Pro Bowl season. In addition, our offensive line—considered a weakness in 1995—had become one of our strong points.

The draft had been good for us, too, as we got cornerback Tom Knight from Iowa in the first round and a hometown boy in quarterback Jake Plummer from Arizona State in the second round.

The Arizona Cardinals players, coaches, management, and fans all expected us to take another step toward playoff contention in 1997. It didn't happen, though.

Another Tough Season

We were hoping for more improvement during the 1997 season, but instead, for the fourth time in my seven years with the team, we finished 4-12.

It was a season with few on-field highlights for the Cardinals.

We started the season with a close loss at Cincinnati, then got our biggest win of the season, a 25-22 overtime decision over the Dallas Cowboys at Sun Devil Stadium. The win snapped the Cowboys' thirteen-game winning streak against us.

It was a huge game for me and for my defensive teammates as we held Michael Irvin, the Cowboys' All-Pro wide receiver, to four receptions and eighteen yards. I didn't have an interception that game and I had only four tackles, but I was named the NFL Defensive Player of the Week. I wanted to share the award with my defensive teammates, especially our front line—and, in particular, Simeon Rice, who had two sacks—which put pressure on Dallas quarterback Troy Aikman all game long.

The win against Dallas would be our last for a while, however, as we went on to lose eight of our next nine to go 2-9. I had some personal highlights along the way, as well as some times when I felt responsible for our losing.

The biggest personal highlight came when I picked off a pass by the New York Giants' Danny Kanell and returned it thirty yards for a touchdown to break a twenty-five-year-old Cardinals team record for touchdown returns, held by Hall of Famer and current team vice president Larry Wilson. Unfortunately, we lost 27-13 at Sun Devil Stadium.

Then there were the lowlights, both for me and for my team.

As much as I felt like my teammates had supported me during our win against the Cowboys, I also felt like I let them down two weeks later in our 19-18 loss to the Buccaneers at Tampa Bay. I'd scored on a 42-yard interception return to give us an 18-12 lead with seconds left in the third quarter, but I was later beaten by Karl Williams for a 31-yard touchdown reception from quarterback Trent Dilfer with 4:48 left in the game. I later apologized to my teammates for that play. I knew they were out there fighting for the win, and I felt like I'd let them down.

I finished the season with six interceptions and two touchdowns and was once again named a starter in the Pro Bowl. I was grateful for the personal success, but I still wanted to win as much as ever—especially after the improvements we'd made in 1996—and what made the losing all the harder to take is that we were so close to being winners.

Falling Just Short

It was incredible how many close games the Arizona Cardinals lost in 1997. In the first eight games of the season alone, we lost two games by one point, 19-18 at Tampa Bay and 20-19 at home to Minnesota; two by three points—24-21 at Cincinnati and 13-10 at Philadelphia; and one by six points, 19-13 at Washington. That's five losses by a total of fourteen points!

It's hard to explain how a team could so consistently lose close games the way we did in 1997. One explanation could be that we haven't learned how to win yet. By that I mean that we know how to play and how to compete, but we don't know what it takes to finish what we've started.

Our next step as a team is to learn how to respond when a game is on the line and when a big play needs to be made. We have to learn to approach those situations without fear, without being afraid to fail or to succeed. I know we have the ability to do that—if we learn how.

And as we grow as men and as football players, we're learning what it takes right now.

Growing into Winners

Winning a Super Bowl championship is a goal of mine just as much as it is for any player in the NFL. We all play with the goal of having a chance to go out and prove that we're the best team in the league. I believe we can accomplish that goal in Phoenix, and there's nothing I would like more than to build on what we have now to where we have a chance to play for the Super Bowl championship.

I love the challenge that is in that way of thinking. I love knowing that I can be part of the Arizona Cardinals' growth from a team with a losing record into Super Bowl contenders. I know it won't be easy, but to tell you the truth, I wouldn't want it to be, because I know that it would be all the more gratifying to go through learning how to win and how to become a contender.

There's something appealing to me about the thought of building from scratch and making a winner out of a team that had been a loser. There's something appealing about a group of men sticking together through the tough times and learning what it takes to be winners. Learning to respect one another and rely on one another on the field. Learning how to win. Together.

The difference between winning and losing in the National Football League isn't based solely on talent. Sometimes, it's more subtle than that. I've seen what most people consider the most talented teams in the world fall flat on their faces, and I've seen teams that might be considered less talented go out and do great things on the field.

The difference, I believe, is what's in the hearts and minds of the players. The difference is *knowing* you can be a winner right where you are.

Heading in the Right Direction

While it would be premature for anyone to suggest that the Arizona Cardinals will be a Super Bowl contender in 1998, I believe this season could be the beginning of some great things for us on the football field.

Although we took a step backward in 1997 as far as wins and losses are concerned, I believe—as do a lot of other people—that we're a team headed in the right direction.

We have a lot of good, young players who are going to get nothing but better as time goes on. One of those players is second-year quarterback Jake Plummer. Although Jake is young and still learning what it takes to be a successful NFL quarterback, I believe he has what it takes to help make the Cardinals winners. He has that air of confidence about him, that attitude that even when things don't go the way he wants them to, he can make himself and his teammates winners. He is exactly the kind of quarterback this team needs.

Although we lost some quality free agents—Kevin Williams, Kent Graham, Michael Bankston, and Eric Hill have left to sign with other teams—Cardinals management has signed some good players this season, including offensive guard Lester Holmes and running back Mario Bates. They also acquired kick returner/receiver Eric Metcalf, the son of former Cardinals great Terry Metcalf, and linebacker Patrick Sapp from the San Diego Chargers as part of a deal to swap first-round draft picks in 1998. In addition, they acquired 1,000-yard rusher Adrian Murrell from the Jets in a pre-draft trade. They have also signed some of our key players to long-term deals, giving us some stability in the coming years.

In addition, we had one of the best drafts of any team in 1998, taking All-American defensive end Andre Wadsworth of Florida State with the third overall pick. We also took defensive back Corey Chavous of Vanderbilt and 6-foot-7, 355-pound offensive tackle Anthony Clement of Southwest Louisiana in the second round of the draft.

The 1998 offseason was a good one for the Arizona Cardinals, and I'm feeling optimistic about where we're headed.

A Submitted Football Player

While I liked the direction the Cardinals were headed as we moved toward the start of the 1998 training camp, I'm also aware that I have a personal responsibility to God, to my team, and to the Cardinal management.

My responsibility is to continue to submit myself to doing the things that those who are paid to solve our team's problems—the coaches and the management—ask me to do. My job, the job God has called me to do at this time in my life, is to play cornerback for the Arizona Cardinals and to do it to the best of my ability.

God has called me to submit to the authority of my coaches and team management, and He's called me to do that in a way that sets an example for my teammates. God has shown me that it is better to lead through example than to tell someone how something should be done. I've learned that if I want someone to do something, they're more likely to do it if I come alongside them and do it with them. For example, if I want to see my teammates work hard, I work hard myself.

I get teased at practice and at team meetings sometimes about going what some of my teammates think is "a little overboard" when it comes to how hard I work. I've even had guys yell out things like, "Hey, Aeneas, don't you have time to get in a few more wind sprints?" when they spied me standing still for a moment.

I enjoy the good-natured ribbing, but I also enjoy knowing that my teammates see me as someone who puts in his best effort—every day in practice and every Sunday in the games. I enjoy knowing that they respect me for my hard work.

While it's true that most of the time I work harder than the coaches ask me to work, there is a reason for it. First of all, I don't want to waste any of the time God has given me. I want to use the time to become the best I can be. The way I see it, God put me in the NFL for—by eternal standards—a fleeting moment, and I've got to make the best of the time He has given me. I also work as hard as I do so that I can be an example to my teammates. I want them to look at me and feel challenged by what they see.

There's another reason I work so hard, though. Sure, I want to set an example of hard work to my teammates, but I also want them to see that I am completely submitted to those in authority over me, in this case the Arizona Cardinals coaching staff. I never want to give anyone reason to believe that I'm not giving the coaches every ounce of effort they ask of me—and more.

God has called me to do my job in a way that is pleasing to Him. That includes giving it the best effort I have, but it also includes giving those in authority over me—my coaches—the respect they deserve as the ones God has placed over me while I wear a Cardinals uniform.

I'm committed to doing just that.

That, in the eyes of my God, is what makes me a winner.

PASS COVERAGE

1. What do you do when there's disappointment in your life?

2. Do you think God cares if a particular football team wins or loses? Why or why not?

3. How important is it to you that you give your best effort in all that you do? How important is it to God?

4. What are the advantages of submitting to those in authority over you? What are the disadvantages?

CHAPTER TEN

EVERYBODY NEEDS A COACH

SUBMIT YOURSELF!

If any of you lacks wisdom, he should ask God, who gives generously to all
without finding fault, and it will be given to him.
—JAMES 1:5

t's amazing to me when I think about the things God has allowed me to accomplish as a member of the Arizona Cardinals, on the football field as well as off.

On the field, I was named the 1991 NFC Defensive Rookie of the Year. Since then, I've been selected to four Pro Bowls (and counting, I hope) and been named All Pro four times. I had twenty-seven interceptions in four years (1994–97) and thirty-eight in my seven seasons in the league.

Off the field, God has allowed me to minister mightily to my teammates and to those in my community. I've had the privilege of seeing people saved, people rededicate their lives to Jesus Christ, marriages healed, and lives turned around. The best part of that is seeing that God used me.

I praise God and give Him the glory for allowing me to do the things I have in the past seven years. I thank Him for allowing me to see the value of submitting all that I am and all that I do to Him.

I know there's no way I could have accomplished what I have without fully submitting myself to God and to the earthly authorities He's placed over me. And there's no way I could have learned that vital aspect of my faith without the help of the authority figures in my life. From my mom and dad, to my high school teachers and coaches, to my college coaches, to the coaching staff with the Arizona Cardinals, I've been blessed with strong authority figures. God used them all in my life, too.

There is a special friend, though, that made as big an impact on my spiritual life as anyone I've ever known. He's a man who taught me about holy living, about the importance of the Word of God in my life, and why I needed to have a heart that is submitted to the things of God.

He's my Coach.

Reunited with an Old Friend

I've learned in my Christian walk that if you're willing to submit to the teaching of someone—someone with more years or more experience in the faith—then God will bring someone like that into your life to help you.

He did it for me.

I first got to know Alfred Picou—I call him "Coach"—when he coached a Little League baseball team I played on when I was a kid. I liked Coach from the time I met him, because I could see that he was the kind of man who liked kids and cared about them. I could tell that he genuinely cared about me, and he was always a source of encouragement for me.

As I got older—as college and other concerns of life took the place of childhood activities like baseball—I pretty much fell out of contact with Coach Picou. I hadn't seen him for years, but one day—at a strategic point in my life—God brought us together.

I had just completed my first year in the NFL, and I had a lot of questions about my faith. I was faced with a lot of temptations I hadn't faced before, and I didn't know what to do to overcome them. On top of that, Tracy and I were dating, and we were faced with some incredible temptations as well as questions about when we would get married.

My heart was at war with my flesh. Because the Spirit of God dwelled within me, I wanted to do what was right in the sight of God. At the same time, though, I was dealing with the temptations. I knew I didn't want to be a hypocrite or a backslider. I wanted to move forward in my relationship with Jesus and to become the kind of man He wanted me to be. I wanted to win

handled the situation the way God wanted me to, so I asked Coach what I should do.

Coach Picou started by assuring me that God wanted to use me in the lives of my friends and family. He went on to tell me that the devil's top purpose for the persecution was to sidetrack me, to make me focus on the negative things people were saying *about* me and not on what God was saying *to* me. If I allowed that to happen, Coach warned me, it could cause me to lose my boldness and to retreat from my witness to my family.

Coach encouraged me to continue doing just what I had been doing—living out my faith in front of my friends and family and praying daily for their salvation. He also told me that I should expect some resistance from my friends and family when I talked about the things of God and not to be discouraged when it came.

A Challenging Coach

Coach not only encouraged me, he challenged me. He challenged me to submit myself to the Word of God and what it had to say about my Christian life.

Coach wasn't a Milquetoast kind of guy. He is a very straightforward person, and if he thinks you need to hear something, he says it. He spoke the truth firmly, even when I didn't always want to hear what he was saying.

I didn't always like everything Coach had to say to me, but I knew that he had my best interests in mind. He was concerned about my spiritual growth, and he was willing to risk our friendship by saying what I *needed* to hear and not just what I wanted to hear.

There were times when my flesh ached at hearing what Coach had to say. For example, he talked to me about getting away from some friends who were negative influences on my life. That was the last thing I wanted to hear. He was talking about some close friends whose company I had enjoyed for years.

It seemed like there wasn't an aspect of my life that Coach and I didn't talk about, and that included my relationship with the most important woman in my life: Tracy.

Should I or Shouldn't I?

I had been dating Tracy for about three years when I came into contact with Coach, and that was good timing, too, because I needed his advice when it came to getting ready to get married.

I told Coach that I felt like I was ready to get married, but that I was still feeling a little fearful about the prospect. I knew that Tracy was the one I wanted to marry. I had prayed about whether I was to marry her and I knew she was the one God had sent for me.

I also told him that Tracy and I had been dealing with sexual temptation (one thing I knew I didn't have to pray about was whether I should fornicate), and we had wondered if it would be, as the 1 Corinthians 7:9 puts it, "better to marry than to burn."

I was ready and willing to do what Coach told me to do, whether it meant waiting, getting married soon, or ending the relationship. I was submitted to his authority over me as the one who was discipling me, and I was willing to do as he said.

"What do you think, Coach?" I asked him.

Coach Picou, true to his form, made it simple for me.

"Well, Aeneas, if you believe she's the one, what are you waiting for?" he asked me. "What's the problem?"

I didn't have an answer for that question. I loved Tracy and I knew she was the one for me. The only problem I had was the fear of the unknown. I'd never been married before, and neither had Tracy. These were uncharted waters for both of us, and I had no idea what to expect in marriage. That was scary for me.

Coach Picou put my fears in perspective, pointing out that the only thing I was afraid of was the change I was thinking of making, and that I shouldn't let that kind of fear stop me from doing anything—even getting married.

Coach gave me just the words I needed that day. He went on to say that if I knew that Tracy was the one for me, don't wait to get engaged, but go ahead and do it.

That's exactly what I did.

A Coach with Authority

What made my relationship with Coach so beneficial to me in the long run wasn't as much that he gave me good advice—which he did—as it was that I purposed in my heart to make him a spiritual authority figure in my life. I didn't have to make Coach Picou an authority figure in my life, but I'm glad God gave me enough sense to do it. On my own, I'm sure I would have tried to go it alone.

I didn't reject Coach's authority, no matter how much of what he said made me uncomfortable or angry. As a young Christian at that point in my life, Coach Picou was exactly what I needed.

What's more, I believe *everybody* needs a Coach.

I've come to the point in my walk with the Lord where I believe it's absolutely crucial to have one person to whom you are accountable and to whom you go when you have questions about your walk with God or about His written Word. I believe it's important for a believer to have that foundation built in his or her life. Furthermore, I think that's backed up in the Bible, including the Book of 2 Timothy, which is a letter of encouragement from the apostle Paul to the young pastor Timothy.

Don't Go It Alone!

We all need instruction in how to submit ourselves to the will of God. Sadly, there are too many young people today whose pride won't allow them to submit to any kind of authority. They have bought into that spirit of independence that permeates our society, the spirit that says, "I can do it myself!" In Christian circles, it's an attitude that says, "As long as I have God, I don't need anyone else!"

That "Lone Ranger" mentality is more the norm than the exception, but it's also a way of thinking that is as wrong and as poisonous as it is common. It's a stubborn, prideful attitude that keeps many young Christians today from living in the fullness of God, simply because they choose to live in their ignorance.

I think it's sad when a young Christian isn't able to submit himself to the discipline of someone who is older and wiser. I've seen it in people I've known, including a friend who had the very same opportunity to grow that I had with Coach Picou. He could have received the same kind of teaching that I did, but he counted the cost to himself and decided he didn't want it.

The Bible says in Ephesians 5:21 that we are to "Submit to one another out of reverence for Christ." The wisdom behind that is this: We need one another. The Bible tells us that we need one another for support, encouragement, and admonition.

I got all those things in large doses from Coach Picou. He supported me in my efforts to do the things I needed to do, encouraged me when I felt overwhelmed, and reprimanded (admonished) me when I stepped out of line.

When I look back on the challenges I faced at that time in my life, I can't help but wonder where I'd be without the firm, loving, sometimes tough guidance I got from Coach Picou. I wonder where I'd be if God hadn't placed within me the will to submit to Coach, the authority figure He brought into my life for the purpose of helping me build a strong foundation to my faith.

Would I be walking in faith as strongly as I am now? Would I understand the importance of prayer, study of the Word, and fellowship? Would I be married to a woman who is the perfect wife for me and the perfect mother for my daughter? For that matter, would I be playing in the National Football League? That's hard to say. Sure, God can do anything through anybody He chooses. If Coach hadn't come along, the Lord may have brought somebody else into my life to do the job. But without that God-given will to submit to Coach Picou's authority in my life, I would probably have missed out on the blessings that I've received because of Coach's teaching.

Authority: Respect Is Due!

It breaks my heart to think that there are so many Christians out there who sell themselves short because they won't submit themselves to the authority that God has placed in their lives. In fact, there are a lot of us who don't even understand the importance of submitting to God Himself!

If people only understood how much God loves them and how much He wants to use authority figures in their lives to give them guidance, support, and encouragement, they'd beg Him for strong authority figures in their lives. They'd beg for a Coach of their own.

I think of myself as a living example of how God can bless someone who knows the value of respect for authority. I know beyond a shadow of a doubt that I wouldn't be where I am today if I didn't understand the importance of submission to those God has placed in authority over me.

I've seen many, many young players—some of them far more talented than I am—who came into the National Football League but couldn't grasp that concept. I've gotten to the point now where when I see someone with that attitude that I know it's only a matter of time before they're out the door, branded as "malcontent" or "uncoachable." I've even tried to help several young guys with that attitude understand that what they're doing has been tried before and that it's a dead-end street. I've tried to tell them that they're paving their own road out of the league when they come in with the "I'll do it my way" attitude.

More than that, I try to show them by example the importance of submission to those in authority.

This Is How It's Done!

I've been blessed with four trips to the Pro Bowl and a long list of postseason All-Pro honors, but I'm still submitted to those who are in authority over me, my coaches. I've been tempted from time to time to change the way I approach things, but I'm happy to say that God has continually reminded me that I'm still to be in submission to those who are in authority over me. It is that understanding that got me where I am as a football player.

It's that understanding that got me where I am in my relationship with God.

As you read this, you might be tempted to think that you can get away with rebelling against the authority figures God has placed in your life. Well,

I guarantee you it won't work. The Bible says in Romans 13 that earthly authorities are put in place by God to act as a covering, to protect you from the enemy. When you step out from under that authority, you are placing yourself in the devil's territory and you're fair game for the enemy.

As you read this book, do you wonder what kinds of blessings you're missing out on because you can't—because you won't—submit yourself to your own personal "Coach"? Do you struggle with the idea of putting yourself under someone's authority, thinking you can go it alone?

If you think that way, you're not alone. In fact, welcome to the human race! Rebelling against authority is part of our fallen, sinful nature. In fact, it *is* our fallen, sinful nature. There is a part in each of us that wants to resist the authority that is over us—especially when that authority is from someone who is helping us grow in our spiritual lives.

Romans 7:21 says that, "When I want to do good, evil is right there with me." Paul wrote this passage to describe the inner conflict he had in wanting to do what was pleasing to God. He recognized that although in his spirit he wanted to do good, his flesh was there with him, wanting to do evil, wanting to rebel.

Even the apostle Paul—the man who wrote most of the epistles in the New Testament—struggled with sinful, rebellious feelings. But he did what I want you to do if you are dealing with the same thing: he looked to Jesus Christ, the most submitted, humble person who ever walked the face of the earth.

A Man of Submission

Jesus was submitted to His family, His teachers, and, most of all, to God. He was submitted to the point where He was willing to do anything it took to please His heavenly Father, even give Himself up to die a horrible, grisly death.

There has never been a man who was as submitted as Jesus. He submitted Himself to the will of God in every conceivable way, starting with leaving His Father's side in heaven to come to earth to dwell among a world full of sinners. He submitted Himself to living a humble life on this earth, a life where He lived day-to-day relying on God the Father for everything. He was submitted to the will of God the Father to the point where He—the Creator of the universe—allowed Himself to be mocked, cursed, beaten, spat upon, then nailed to a cross.

There's an old hymn that says, "He could have called ten thousand angels to destroy the world and set him free." There's no doubt He could have done just that. But He didn't. He couldn't. He had come to this earth for a purpose, and that purpose was to fulfill the will of the Father. He said it best as He knelt in the garden, the prospect of what lay before Him crushing down on Him literally like the weight of the world, when He looked toward heaven and said, "My Father, if it is not possible for this cup to be taken away unless I drink it, may your will be done" (Matthew 26:42).

Jesus didn't just tell His followers to submit to God, He showed them how in the way that He lived and in the way He died. He was in every way an example of what we are to be as His children.

If you have a hard time submitting to those in authority over you, look to Jesus Christ. He showed the perfect way. He was the perfect example of how a man of respect can also be a man who is completely submitted.

Find Yourself a Coach

You can't go wrong when you act in obedience to God's Word and submit yourself to the earthly authorities He has placed over you. When you do that, you are afforded all the protection and all the blessings God wants to give you.

On the other hand, when you rebel against God's authority, you put yourself at odds with God's will, and when you're at odds with God's will, you remove yourself from His protective covering. Then, you're on your own! That's not a very safe place to be!

God wants our full submission, first to Him, then to the authority structures He's placed over us. The great thing about that is that it's *for our own good!*

The bottom line, though, is that it's our choice. God won't force us to submit to Him and He won't force you to submit to the authorities He's placed over you.

I can tell you, though, that there's no better life than one that's submitted completely to the will of God. I'm a living, breathing example of what God can do in the life of a man who humbles himself and submits himself to God's will!

PASS COVERAGE

1. What is the purpose of authority in the life of a believer?

2. What does it mean to you to submit?

3. Is it easy for you to submit to authority, or do you struggle with that concept?

4. What are some of the authority structures God has placed in your life?

AN AENEAS WILLIAMS PROFILE

Personal

- Aeneas was born January 29, 1968, in New Orleans, Louisiana, to Lawrence and Lillian Williams. He has two older brothers: Malcolm and Achilles.

- Aeneas and wife, Tracy, have one daughter, Saenea ("Aeneas" spelled backwards).

- Hometown: Phoenix, Arizona.

- Attended Alcee Fortier High School in New Orleans, where he played football for three years. Named All-District and New Orleans High School Most Valuable Player his senior year.

- Played high school football with or against future NFL players Ashley Ambrose, Maurice Hurst, Kevin Lewis, Michael Lindsey, and Garry Lewis.

College

- Participated in student government in college, serving as freshman senator and sophomore class vice president, at Southern University in Baton Rouge, Louisiana, where his father and brother Achilles attended.

- Didn't play football his first two years in college, but walked on and became starter during his junior year in college. Played three years at Southern.

- Named First Team All-Southwestern Athletic College Player in 1989 and 1990.

- Named Sheridan All-America in 1989 and 1990 and Sheridan Black College All-America Defensive Most Valuable Player in 1990.

- Named All-Louisiana First Team in 1989 and 1990.

- Named Black College All-America in 1989 and 1990.

- Shared national lead (with Claude Pettaway of Maine) in interceptions with eleven during his senior football season in 1990.

- Finished college career with 228 tackles, twenty interceptions, and twenty-five pass deflections in three seasons at Southern.

- Graduated with 3.2 grade-point average in accounting in the spring of 1990.

College Statistics*

Season	GP	UT	AT	TT	FR	INT	DFL	S
1988	9	24	31	55	1	2	3	2.5
1989	11	45	39	84	2	7	5	0
1990	11	43	36	79	0	11	17	0
Totals	31	122	106	228	3	20	25	2.5

Statistics courtesy of Southern University Sports Information Department.

Aeneas in the NFL

- Selected by the Phoenix Cardinals in the third round (59th pick overall) of the 1991 NFL draft, then signed with Cardinals on July 26.

- Had an interception and four pass deflections in first NFL game, a 24-14 Cardinals win over the Los Angeles Rams in Anaheim.

- Named NFL Players Association NFC Defensive Rookie of the Year after recording NFC leading (tied with Deion Sanders and Tim McKyer of Atlanta and Ray Crockett of Detroit) six interceptions in 1991 season. First rookie cornerback to lead NFC in interceptions since Dallas' Everson Walls in 1981.

- Consensus All-Rookie Selection in 1991.

- Named starter in Pro Bowl following 1994, '95, '96, and '97 seasons.

- Consensus all-pro recognition from Associated Press, *College and Pro Football Newsweekly, Pro Football Weekly*, the Pro Football Writers Association, *The Sporting News,* and *USA Today* following 1995, 1996, and 1997 seasons. Named all-NFC by *Football News* and United Press International the same season.

- Has never missed a game in seven-year NFL career.

Career NFL Statistics*

Year	Team	G/GS	TT	PD	INT	YDS	TDI	FF	FR	TDF	S
1991	Phoe.	16/15	48	17	6	60	0	0	2	0	0
1992	Phoe.	16/16	48	13	3	25	0	0	1	0	0
1993	Phoe.	16/16	42	15	2	87	1	0	2	1	0
1994	Ariz.	16/16	41	28	9	89	0	0	1	0	0
1995	Ariz.	16/16	62	22	6	86	3	0	3	1	0
1996	Ariz.	16/16	77	18	6	89	1	0	1	0	1
1997	Ariz.	16/16	63	17	6	95	2	1	0	0	0
Totals		112/111	381	130	38	531	7	1	10	2	1

Statistics courtesy of Arizona Cardinals.

Keys to abbreviations—G/GS: games played/games started. TT: total tackles. PD: passes defensed. INT: interceptions. YDS: interception return yards.

TDI: interception returns for touchdown. FF: forced fumbles. FR: fumbles recovered. TDF: fumble returns for touchdown. S: sacks.

Inside the Numbers

Statistically, Aeneas Williams ranks as one of the finest defensive backs in the game. Here is how he ranks with some of the best active defenders in the NFL as of the end of the 1997 season:

Career Interceptions

Player	No.
Eugene Robinson	49
Darrell Green	44
Rod Woodson	41
Albert Lewis	40
Eric Ellen	39
Eugene Daniel	38
Kevin Ross	38
Aeneas Williams	38
Lionel Washington	37
2 tied with	36

Career Int. Ret. TD's

Player	No.
Deion Sanders	7
Darrell Green	6
Aeneas Williams	6
Rod Woodson	5
Terry McDaniel	5
Eric Allen	5
Darryll Lewis	5
Otis Smith	5
5 tied with	4

Career Defensive TD's

Player	No.
Deion Sanders	8
Darrell Green	8
Terry McDaniel	7
Aeneas Williams	7
Rod Woodson	6
Anthony Parker	6
7 tied with	5

Career Int. Ret. Yards

Player	Yds.
Deion Sanders	941
Rod Woodson	860
Eugene Robinson	719
Kevin Ross	654
Terry McDaniel	624
Tim McDonald	600
Eric Allen	570
Darryl Williams	557
Tyrone Braxton	545
Aeneas Williams	531

In only seven seasons, Aeneas already ranks as one of the best defensive backs in Cardinals history. Here is how he compares:

Career Interceptions

Player	No.
Larry Wilson	52
Roger Wehrli	40
Aeneas Williams	38
Dick Lane	30
Pat Fischer	29

Career Interception Ret. for TD.

Player	No.
Aeneas Williams	6
Larry Wilson	5
Robert Massey	3
Bill Blackburn	3
Pat Fischer	3

Season Int. Ret. for TD.

Player, season	No.
Robert Massey, 1992	3
Aeneas Williams, 1995	2
Aeneas Williams, 1997	2
Larry Wilson, 1966	2
Pat Fischer, 1964	2
Jerry Norton, 1961	2
Bill Stacy, 1961	2
Billy Blackburn, 1948	2